To John and Diana,
who taught us about the
power of love.

We also dedicate this book to Dr. Scott Strahlman, Stasia's pediatrician, for his availablility at all hours, his belief in us and what we were trying to accomplish, his efforts on our behalf that definitely went above and beyond the call of duty, and for making March 11, 1990 just a little bit easier.

To Dr. Shaukat Ashai, our friend, for his unequivocal support and courage during my pregnancy; a crucial time not only in our lives but little Stasia's as well. We are so glad it was you God chose to deliver the news that would break our hearts.

To Maybian Gloth, Stasia's primary nurse on Dr. Freeman's floor, whose listening ear and gentle, loving, Christian counsel saw us through many a rough spot and sleepless night.

To Janie Appler and all the other many nurses that we were so privileged to work with and rely on at Johns Hopkins whose names are too numerous to list here but are written in our memory and on our hearts forever.

To Lil Price, truly an angel of mercy handpicked by the good Lord to accompany us on the single most difficlut journey of our lives and undisputedly our greatest test of faith. We have often remarked that if we had opened the door to our home on the day you first arrived one second sooner, we know we would have caught the good Lord Himself creating you right there on our front steps out of the dust of the earth to adopt us, to love us, to guide and support us, to cry with us, and at long last to rejoice with us. It was you and your Christlike qualities of Christian service that first set Alsie on the path to pursuing a career in nursing.

To our many friends at Chapelgate Church whose faithful prayers and loving presence supported us through the entire journey.

To Dr. Lane Adams and his family for keeping the Spirit of God alive in our lives despite Alsie's frequent seeming need to "kill the messenger." What courage and persistence God has blessed you all with!

To Pauline Chisholm whose tireless efforts on our behalf provided the lifeline we so desperately needed with our church family.

To Reverend Ron Steel and his wife Jenny, who adopted us the day after Stasia went home to be with the Lord and allowed us to practically take up residency in their home and their lives. Thank you for being so generous with your most valuable treasures—yourselves, your time, and your family. We do not exaggerate when we state that we would never have survived that first year alone without your love.

To Alsie's mother, who was so unselfish with both her time and her prayers as we were adjusting to our new role as parents.

To Dave and Betty Bower who provided some semblance of narmalcy to our lives as parents. They never

Stasia's Gift

Stasia's Gift

Brian and Alsie Kelley
with Mark Littleton

CROSSWAY BOOKS • WHEATON, ILLINOIS
A DIVISION OF GOOD NEWS PUBLISHERS

Stasia's Gift.

Copyright © 1993 by Brian and Alsie Kelley and Mark Littleton

Published by Crossway Books
  a division of Good News Publishers
  1300 Crescent Street
  Wheaton, Illinois 60187.

Cover illustration: Ron DiCianni

Art Direction/Design: Mark Schramm

First printing, 1993

Printed in the United States of America

ISBN 0-89107-703-0

Library of Congress Cataloging-in-Publication Data
Kelley, Brian, 1952-
  Stasia's gift / Brian and Alsie Kelley, with Mark Littleton.
    p. cm.
  1. Consolation. 2. Mental retardation—Religious aspects.
3. Kelley, Alsie, 1952- . 4. Kelley, Brian, 1952- . I. Kelley,
Alsie, 1952- .II. Littleton, Mark, 1950- . III. Title.
BV4907.K45 1993   248.8'6—dc20   92-44002
ISBN 0-89107-703-0

01		00		99		98		97		96		95		94		93
15	14	13	12	11	10	9	8	7	6	5	4	3	2	1

missed a holiday on which to send Stasia a card and some encouraging words for her parents. We gratefully acknowledge that without their efforts, this book would never have been written.

And most importantly, to Brian's parents and Alsie's adopted family, the Kelleys who were singlehandedly responsible for seeing to it that our precious little daughter never ever wanted for anything. Never were two people more adept at loving a grandchild. Without your love and encouragement, your time and your generosity so that Stasia could have the best of everything, we would not have the peace that God has so richly bestowed on us today. Few people in this world are so fortunate.

We also dedicate this book to the legion of men and women, doctors and nurses, friends and family without whose love, support, understanding, compassion and encouragement this book could never have been written; it would have been a very different story indeed.

Contents

First Signs of
a Problem

THE SONOGRAM WAS TAKING FAR LONGER than usual. The technician, Pam, peered at the screen and kept furrowing her brow with concern. It was my third sonogram in three months.

I'd discovered I was pregnant in mid-1986. I had experienced some spotting, and my obstetrician, Dr. Skaukat Ashai, wanted to check everything out through several tests, including an amniocentesis. My husband, Brian, and I simply wanted to ensure that everything was well, and that if it wasn't, Dr. Ashai would have time to correct any problems before they got worse.

I'm not one to clam up under such circumstances. I finally spoke, swallowing away the tremor in my voice. "Is something wrong?"

I had come to know Pam as an incredibly gentle and patient person. She was especially understanding and took a real interest in our situation, always asking questions about any progress and expressing interest and compassion about our struggle to conceive. All of that drew us to one another. She always encouraged me about it.

She answered my question by saying, "I really can't answer that.

You'll have to talk to the doctor." She was intense and concentrated, with long silences as she took various measurements, and finally I relaxed and simply drifted in my thoughts. In a short time I fell asleep.

It had taken Brian and me seven years to reach this moment. During that time we underwent every fertility test we'd heard of, and many more we hadn't. In many ways, the whole process had been humiliating to me—the product of the "perfect" upper middle class upbringing at an exclusive girl's school called Wroxeter-on-the-Severn. My father had been a Circuit Court judge until he died of a heart attack at the age of forty-two in 1968. When Spiro Agnew was chosen as Richard Nixon's running mate, my dad was considered to be the governor's possible replacement. The heart attack struck as we were planning a boat trip to the annual Seafood Festival in Annapolis, Maryland. He slipped into a coma as I cradled his head in my arms. He died less than an hour later. I was sixteen years old.

So much of my later life pivoted on that moment. Up until that point I had been pampered and protected, but suddenly I felt totally abandoned. I felt deeply angry and resentful because the one person who'd provided direction and substance for my life was gone. I stumbled along in my adult life, attending four different colleges, without any clear purpose in life. All of my childhood security was bound up in knowing that my father had all the answers. I remember thinking I would never need to worry about anything in life because he had worked it out so perfectly in advance. I envisioned that my whole life would truly be perfect, because all I had to do was ask Dad and he'd provide the answer.

Then I met Brian in 1979 at the age of twenty-seven, and suddenly things began coming together for me again. Life got back "on track." We were two very lonely people who in coming together became instant soulmates, best friends. There was a wonderful security in one another that we hadn't found in careers or in anything else. We both wanted a family, even a large family, and we talked about it constantly. As a Navy "brat," Brian's family had moved a dozen times before he graduated from high school. My own experience in losing my father motivated me to want to recreate an imagined "Norman Rockwell" kind of intimacy, union and security.

We both wanted children, and we wanted to give them everything of the best we could afford—a secure, loving home with doting, involved parents and an atmosphere of complete acceptance. As Brian rose in his position as regional controller for a hotel chain, plus his preparations for becoming a CPA at the University of Baltimore, plus my having my own word processing business, it all looked not only possible but probable.

How many times had Brian and I sat together in the evening after work and talked about the children we were convinced we'd have in due time! We batted around names. We talked about schools the children would attend, vacation spots we'd visit, and on and on. We had it all planned out.

"Of course, he'll go to a private school," I'd say, and would then list several in the Baltimore area: St. Timothy's, McDonogh, Bryn Mawr.

Inevitably Brian would smile as if chiding me. "He?"

"Or she," I would answer quickly.

I don't know what goes on in other mothers' minds as they contemplate that first little life they long to bring into the world. For me it was a lifelong dream. Even as a child, my nickname among some of my classmates was "the little mother," because I was always showing special help and concern for anyone who got hurt in a game or was simply upset for whatever reason.

I wanted a family—hordes of kids in the yard, yelling, screaming, jumping around, playing tug-of-war, rolling around in the sandbox, swinging up to touch the stars on a backyard playset, but of course always well-behaved and perfect little adults when the occasion required. I longed to take trips and show them the world, to relive hundreds of little discoveries through them, to open

Christmas packages and see their eyes light up, to plan huge 4th of July pcnics, to have birthday parties and watch them blow out the candles with that glimmer of joy in their eyes. I had many fears about being a good mother, but putting that aside, I wanted children, little ones, especially babies. Brian and I had an agreement: I would raise them for the first six years, and then he would take them until they were twenty-one and properly behaved. I wanted the whole thing, every blessing of God. Our pastor, Dr. Lane Adams, had assured us God would soon bless us in that regard, and we had all prayed together countless times about it.

For the last two months I'd been on an incredible high that I'd finally gotten pregnant. It seemed as if God had answered all our prayers. But now as Pam scrutinized the sonogram screen, I was fearful that our dreamworld would be shattered.

Because I was thirty-five years old, both Brian and I knew this was a high-risk pregnancy. That was part of the reason for the test in the first place. Dr. Ashai wanted "to cover all the bases," and we were in complete agreement.

Despite the risks involved, though, we believed God was in the process of blessing us beyond our highest dreams. Here was the first proof: after five years of pain and prayer, I'd conceived. As always, my mind stated the obvious truth: God was "with us" again.

This is a difficult thing for me to say even now, because for those long years before my pregnancy two events haunted both Brian and me. They are memories that I can only write about with tears, but they shaped both of us and made us what we are today.

At the age of twenty-four, scared, unmarried, and pregnant, I went to the Planned Parenthood Center in Baltimore alone, asked a few questions, and was told the thing inside me was "just a mass of tissue," certainly not a genuine human being. I remember that lonely walk down a cold corridor, my body just covered by the slit-up-the-back hospital gown. It was all over in a matter of minutes. Several friends and Planned Parenthood assured me I had done the done the sensible thing, the responsible thing. It was all part of the new freedom and "right" we women had won in *Roe v. Wade* at the price of years of fighting and legal battling.

Nonetheless, from the beginning I had felt uncomfortable and had doubts that I was doing the right thing. A thought kept clawing away inside me: was that three-month-old "thing" inside me really just "a mass of tissue"?

Over the next few years I became obsessed with that question. I wondered if others felt the guilt and remorse that I felt. To read the news then and to study the political and medical "facts" being given even today, many would have us believe there are "no psychological, physical or other aftereffects" from undergoing that procedure. But for me the answers to the questions, Was it right?, Was it the only choice?, Were there other options?, Did anyone else feel like me? haunted me constantly.

I finally searched for books that would spell out what happened inside a pregnant woman. Despite years of college and a sophisticated, worldly lifestyle, I was horribly ignorant about the whole subject. A nurse gave me a book called *Our Bodies, Our Selves*. In it were charts and pictures of the whole process of a baby's development from conception to birth. At twelve days. At one month. At two months. Etc.

Even now I relive that terrible moment when I came to the picture of an unborn child at three months, the same age as my baby I had aborted. My reaction to the image was instantaneous, paralyzing, crushing. To me, the unborn child looked inescapably human, with tiny arms and legs, a head, a heart. It was a tiny human being, nothing close to the "mass of tissue" I was told it was.

As I stared at the photos, I was numb. In my heart of hearts I felt—I *knew*—that I had murdered not only an innocent human being, but my own child.

These memories are my constant companions—whenever I look into the eyes of a newborn baby, whenever I see the joy on a new mother's face. And even today as I write I feel that same remorse even though I know I've been forgiven through Christ. Often over the years I have sat in church or stood staring out my kitchen window and relived that tragedy as if it happened just yesterday, my heart crying out with the same anguish, my mind calculating the age of my "first child" and wondering what she or he would look like and be involved in if alive today.

During those years as Brian and I struggled to conceive our first child, I could not escape what I believed was a real possibility: my being punished by God for what I'd done.

Added to this burden was Brian's own experience with abortion. When he was twenty and in college at Southern Connecticut State College, a relationship he'd had with a young woman led to her getting pregnant. It was the winter of 1974, barely a year after the Supreme Court's *Roe v. Wade* decision. Marriage was out of the question for both of them. His girlfriend decided to have an abortion, and Brian took what he knows today was a passive role, offering her no alternatives. He even paid for the operation. Within another year the relationship had disintegrated.

My husband today is a quiet man, with a high sense of moral integrity that I continue to admire. He possesses a quiet inner strength that reins me in gently and persuasively without becoming suffocating as I have seen in other men. He does not express himself as effusively or dramatically as I do in public. But over the years, as our marriage moved from a oneness in body and heart to a oneness in soul, both of us have expressed to each other the depth of our pain over our respective experiences with abortion. While we both believe now in God's grace, love, compassion, and mercy toward those who have sinned, we did not then have the relationship with Christ that we do now, and the sense of forgiveness from God was far from us. We struggled daily with the possibility that our inability to conceive was a direct result of our moral mistakes, and perhaps even a punishment from God.

*

When I awoke on the examining table, Pam was still scrutinizing the screen. As I gazed at her intense expression, I really didn't suspect or believe anything could be wrong. God was blessing us now. What could go wrong? More or less, I just wanted to be reassured. So I repeated the question, "Pam, is there anything wrong?"

She shook her head uncertainly, grimacing and squinting hard at the screen. "I'd rather have you talk to the doctor about it."

There are two things I've always feared—all the way back to my days as a child, ever since I was aware that such things could happen. The first was divorce. I'd seen it happen to several schoolmates and friends. I knew well the insecurity, rejection, and loneliness that resulted. I didn't want that to happen to me, and Brian didn't either. His unwavering commitment to our marriage is a mainstay to my own emotional stability.

My other fear was to give birth to a handicapped child. I could not bear the thought of watching one of my own children experience the ridicule and pain I knew so many handicapped children went through. I tend to be empathetic, at times to the point of pain. Human suffering makes me crazy, and if there were one thing I could give the world, it would be to rid it of all such suffering. This was a fear deep in my psyche, because I thought I understood something of the pain, disillusionment, and trouble such little ones must go through. I honestly did not think I could emotionally survive seeing my own child live through such insecurity and rejection.

Pam continued to work over the computer screen, and I said one more time, "Pam, please tell me . . . Do you see something wrong?"

She looked up, and our eyes met briefly. I sensed she was deeply upset as she said, "The ventricles are definitely enlarged."

I had no idea what that meant, and she repeated again that we needed to talk to Dr. Ashai.

Moments later we sat down in our obstetrician's office. Brian took my hand and held it. Dr. Ashai is a close personal friend, an excellent physician, and an uncommonly kind man. I had known him many years as one with an uncanny ability to be gentle and compassionate in all circumstances. He looked at both of us and said, "There may be a problem. The sonograms are all showing an enlargement of the ventricles."

I asked what that meant.

"Hydrocephalus, otherwise referred to as water on the brain." He described what the sonogram had pictured. "During normal pregnancy the ventricles enlarge with fluid, then shrink as the brain develops, draining off by way of the spinal column. However, if there's a blockage and the fluid doesn't drain, it puts pressure on the brain. That can cause serious damage."

"How much?" I asked, for the first time praying that his words "may be a problem" were truly a "may be" and not a "definitely."

Dr. Ashai touched my hand. He looked at Brian, then at me. He said, "I want to be honest with you, but there's no way to determine to what degree the brain is being affected until after the baby is born. We'll continue to perform sonograms every two weeks in order to watch the baby's development and monitor the situation. We want to make sure the heart, lungs, and kidneys develop properly and that there's no facial disfiguration. And it could very well be a temporary blockage." He smiled reassuringly, but my woman's intuition detected an anxiety in his eyes that I feared.

I nodded, and Brian's lips trembled with a slight smile. He squeezed my hand and hugged me, then kissed me. "I love you, Alsie Kelley. It'll be okay. You'll see."

✳

Several weeks and sonograms later, Dr. Ashai sat us down in his office for a serious talk. I sensed he was trying to be gentle about it, but I had to appreciate his directness. He told us, "There is an unmistakable enlarging of the ventricles. It's certain hydro-cephalus."

Almost afraid to press on, I finally asked, "What does that mean?"

"The baby has a 50-50 chance of being developmentally disabled. It could mean anything from a mild learning disability to severe mental retardation." Dr. Ashai patiently answered the multitude of questions we had and spent many extra minutes giving us time to think and clear our minds. After a final silence, he said, "Is there anything else?" and we said no. It was something he always asked, and we greatly appreciated it.

Finally he stood and walked to the door. He was upset, though I could see he was trying not to show it. He said, "I'm very sorry about the prognosis. But I want to be straightforward with you. I know you want it that way, too. Would you like to be alone for a moment?"

All I could feel was a deep sense of betrayal. I could not understand how God could do this to us. For all those years, we'd wondered if He was punishing us because of our earlier involvements with abortion. But now that we'd conceived, we were just as convinced He'd answered our prayers at last. And now . . .

As I sat there, a chill hopelessness gripped me. I suddenly remembered my own words only months before when I'd made a vow to God, a kind of foxhole promise to eliminate the problem of possible punishment. I had prayed with utter sincerity, "If You give me another chance, God, I will see it through . . . no matter what."

Suddenly I felt trapped. God had called me on my promise and had not rewarded us with the healthy baby I'd envisioned.

Somehow I turned to Brian. His usually calm, confident eyes looked large and worried behind his glasses. Even his dark brown hair looked slightly gray. I said to him, "Are you willing to see this through?"

Abortion had crossed my mind, but only momentarily. I knew

I would never go that route again. But I didn't know what Brian would say.

Brian paused for several long moments as he searched his own heart and feelings for the right words. Then he said, "Yes."

"Are you certain?"

"Yes."

"Okay . . . If you're sure."

His unflinching responses calmed me. I knew now that we would see it through together. I wouldn't be alone.

In that brief exchange I felt as though some eternal transaction had just occurred and been resolved. Whatever came now, I knew we'd see it through together. And there was still a 50 percent chance that the baby would be close to normal, without any severe handicaps whatsoever.

I didn't know then that what was coming would turn out to be the most spiritually transforming and at the same time the most painful experience of our lives.

Going Back

I WAS BORN ALSIE LUCILLE PITCHER on June 9, 1952. My grandfather had been a Methodist minister in Baltimore and had been on the radio. My father, Paul Pitcher, was a well-known Maryland lawyer and Circuit Court judge in Annapolis. His portrait hangs in the courthouse to this day.

My parents always seemed to be concerned that I excel, that I always be at my best in the eyes of the world. Much of that training has been passed along in my own perfectionistic tendencies. I attended a prominent girls' school in Maryland called Wroxeter-on-the-Severn, run by a disciplined, high-caliber retired Army major who turned out "ladies" and "debs" and sent students to the finest colleges and universities. There were seven graduates in my senior class, all of us supposedly destined for life in the power lanes, to be married to men in medicine, law, the university, and politics. I was protected in many ways that left me naive but outspoken, well-educated but other-worldly, materialistic but longing for an unconditional, accepting love I believed had to be there but which I'd never experienced.

My father was an avid boatman and owned a thirty-eight-foot Chris Craft that we used to explore the Chesapeake Bay and the rivers that flowed into it. As I wrote earlier, he died of a heart attack when I was sixteen, slipping into a coma while in my arms.

That began the worst period in my life. I was set adrift. Dad had always been the "glue" that held our family together, but with his death came a period of uncertainty, insecurity, and lack of purpose that characterized the next eleven years of my life.

I spent the next four years at four different colleges, finally finding what I thought I wanted at the University of West Florida, majoring in pre-law. I thought I might follow in my father's legal footsteps. I supported myself and paid my tuition by working as a waitress in a Sambo's Restaurant. At the time I sensed that I had no "ground zero," no sense of what was right and wrong in an absolute sense. I finally finished school, graduated in 1976 with a B.A. in political science/pre-law, went to work in Charleston, South Carolina, and eventually returned to Maryland.

One fact stuck with me, though, all during that time. In high school I had a close friend named Heidi Gutsche, a fellow student at Wroxeter. Heidi and her family exhibited a vibrant, committed faith in Christ that touched and intrigued me. I had long since stopped attending church, and I had no idea what a personal relationship with Jesus Christ was all about. But Heidi's faith was real, deep, and open. Occasionally she invited me to her home Bible study, where teenagers played guitar and sang, laughed and kidded, and studied the Bible. The closeness of those times always touched me deeply because I had wanted it so badly for so long. Heidi's family was to me a picture of the warmth and love I craved. I remember especially their "family times" after dinner, when they remained seated around the table and discussed the Bible. That projected a sense of unity and love that I envied. More than that, it spoke of a rootedness and family security for which I longed.

During the following years, whenever things got rough I would reach for my Bible and try to arrive at that emotional "place" of peace and safety the Gutsche family had shown me so graphically. I could never quite arrive there, but it comforted me somewhat nevertheless.

I worked various jobs over the years until 1979 when I met Brian.

★

Brian Kelley was born October 27, 1952. His father was a career naval officer. His family pulled up roots every one or two years, and Brian attended twelve schools from elementary through high school.

He graduated from Southern Connecticut State College in 1974 with a B.A. in political science. He worked first for the Army as a civilian, then went back to school through an extension of the University of Virginia and obtained a teaching certificate in high school history. He substituted in the public schools in Virginia and then in Connecticut and began working at night as a hotel desk clerk to supplement his income.

After receiving promotions at the hotel, he quit substitute teaching and decided to pursue a career in the hotel industry. In 1978 he became an internal auditor for American Motor Inns, a chain that owned and operated fifty-five Holiday Inns.

In the spring of 1979 Brian was auditing the Holiday Inn at the BWI Airport in Elkridge, Maryland, for a week. He immediately noticed the new Director of Services—me, later informing me I was beautiful, sophisticated, and precisely the kind of lady he'd occasionally pictured in his dreams as the woman for him. I fended off his first efforts, but he was persistent and repeatedly dropped into my office to "instruct" me on accounting procedures or anything else that came to mind. Wednesday night was "Italian Night" in the hotel restaurant, and he says now he figured this would be another chance to "instruct" me on this important facet of hotel management. He asked me if I'd like to have dinner.

I told him I had to watch my weight, and pasta wasn't the way to do it. Brian answered, "Well, don't eat." He meant, "Come sit with me and watch me eat, enjoy the company, and have a glass of wine while you're at it."

I interpreted his behavior as arrogant. I had already come to think of him as the hotel money "cop" and didn't care one way or the other whether he ate. But his invitation made me mad, so I immediately agreed—just to irk him.

Dinner together was fun, but afterwards I realized he had pumped me for all sorts of information about me and my life, but I knew virtually nothing about him.

A couple of days later—Friday—was Brian's last day, and he had to leave to do an audit at another hotel. He was eating lunch alone, and I managed to walk by and make some caustic remark about "lonely hotel auditors who dine with all their friends by themselves." But he invited me to sit down and said, "So when are you going to go out with me?"

I simply stared back at him. I had a personal policy *never ever* to date someone I worked with, and I never made exceptions. He'd also caught me completely off guard.

The silence dragged on until, unable to stand it any longer, Brian said, "Say something for heaven's sake."

I heard my lips say, "Okay," but my ears were quite astonished.

That night we dined in Little Italy in downtown Baltimore, then went to a lounge for a drink. We spent the rest of the night talking in Brian's car, and before we knew it the sun came up. I suddenly realized that not only had we had a great time, but this time I knew something about him.

Over the next few months we dated every time Brian was in town—which he managed to engineer quite often—and Brian advised me to get out of the hotel business, which I eventually did. We were married a year and half later, on October 11, 1980.

Shortly after we were married, we began to discuss the possibility of having children, and we both decided it was important to raise children in the church. In preparation for this eventuality, we began attending a United Methodist church near our home in

Baltimore, Maryland. This laid a foundation and began a journey which many years later would result in a genuine relationship with Jesus Christ.

A short time later we found our present church home in Chapelgate Presbyterian Church (PCA), at that time located in Ellicott City, Maryland.

*

I have to admit at the outset that both Brian and I are loners and homebodies. We both grew up in families that entertain a great deal and vastly prefer small, intimate dinner parties to larger gatherings. Brian is tall, with a laid-back frame that slips into a contented slouch once ensconced in his chair in the family room of our home. He wears his dark brown hair blown slightly over his forehead and often bends forward when talking to those shorter than his 6'1" stature. Behind his glasses he looks serious, but there's always a ready smile tugging itself to the surface that makes visitors feel liked and listened to. He likes to be precise in his statements and thinks carefully before answering.

I've often told others, "No one would ever think Brian is as strong as he is, because he's so unassuming. He doesn't push himself on anyone." He has an innate strength that I have always admired.

Brian describes me as a firebrand. Maybe it's my father's legal background and the love of courtroom drama, but Brian says I'm a whirl of motion as I talk. I don't much like the picture, but that's how he puts it.

In a nutshell, we're so totally opposite that you'd think we wouldn't get along. My enthusiasm is usually reined in by Brian's gentle comment, "Now it wasn't exactly that way, honey." And Brian will often find himself knee-deep in projects he never even contemplated due to my compulsive nature. But the beautiful thing is that over our twelve years of marriage we have become soulmates, and my love and admiration for him only grows with each passing year.

Stasia

FTER WE LEARNED that our child would possibly have some level of disability, our joy diminished considerably as the terms *handicap* and *mental retardation* became a part of our daily vocabulary. We both knew we would have to live through the next six months in a state of uncertainty, with a slender thread of hope precariously balanced against the fear that our baby would be seriously handicapped. I had not yet told anyone of Dr. Ashai's words, but both Brian and I wondered again if we were being punished for our errors of the past.

In many ways, though, the doctors were optimistic. As they continued monitoring our baby's condition, we learned the child was a girl. I read everything I could on the subject of hydrocephalus, searching for some ray of divine hope that would get me through this. In fact, one well-meaning person insisted God would not allow my baby to be born handicapped—He would most definitely heal her. I replied, "I know God can heal; I just don't know if He will."

Brian and I went about maintaining a sense of normalcy, or at least tried to do so. We attended special cesarean section classes at Columbia Medical Plan. We visited Crib N' Cradle, a well-known local baby products store, to buy a crib, diaper pails, dressers, a rocking chair, coverlets, pillows, quilts, a lamp, and everything else we thought we needed.

At that time something happened that I only remembered much later. Many of our friends and relatives kept up a totally optimistic front about our situation. They assured us it would "all work out" and that there was "nothing to worry about" and so on. The day we went to Crib 'N Cradle, though, while we walked among the long rows of cribs trying to make a decision, an older woman and her pregnant daughter began talking to me. The daughter continued on her way, but the mother and I talked about dressers and rockers, and soon she began to relate to me that her daughter was having a problem pregnancy. She had been told she might give birth to a handicapped child, and she was struggling with a decision about whether to terminate the pregnancy or not.

I sensed this mother was in real turmoil about this, and I empathized with her deeply. I responded with my own story and the problems we were facing and how difficult it had been, but we'd come to the decision to see it through. She said to me, "You certainly seem to be handling it well, and you appear to be a very strong person."

That stunned me. If anything, that was the last thing I felt. Many times I was plagued with nearly overwhelming doubts. I didn't tell her any of this, but perhaps she saw the surprise in my expression, and suddenly she bored in on me intently and said, "God will not give you more than you can handle." She said it with such certainty that Brian in particular, as he overheard it, was amazed. It was such a stark contrast to what everyone else was saying. He interpreted it to mean that the road ahead might be rough, but God would not abandon us. It was a powerfully reassuring moment for him at that time, and he had no idea how often he would recall it in the future. We never saw that woman again.

We consulted a genetic specialist about our options and what might still be done while the baby was in the womb. In the process I came face to face with what I began to perceive as the "medical" attitude toward abortion. After the testing and confirmations of the baby's condition, each doctor would patiently explain the various options. It seemed to come down to two. One, to see the pregnancy through; the other, abortion.

Both Brian and I had already decided option 2 was unthinkable. Yet, each doctor continued to offer the option of abortion as viable. This began to grate on my heart. Why would doctors, who'd vowed to preserve life, continue to suggest this option when we'd so clearly stated this was not a possibility for us? The doctors seemed to offer this option as if there were no moral consequences involved.

At an appointment with still another obstetrician, Dr. Tim Johnson, a specialist in hydrocephalus, I said to him, "Abortion is not now, nor will it ever be an option in this case, doctor. I don't believe I can destroy the gift God has given us even if my child is handicapped. There is no way we will ever consider abortion. I have to give her a chance at life."

My throat suddenly constricted with emotion as I remembered again how easily, over ten years before, I'd come to just the opposite conclusion.

Dr. Johnson quietly gazed at me, then said, "I can't tell you how glad I am to hear that."

"You are?" I was so surprised, his words stunned me. He was the first doctor who'd expressed anything other than a clinical consideration of the options.

Dr. Johnson said, "I have people come in here, and if the baby is male and they want a female or vice versa, they get an abortion. If they want the baby to have blond hair and it's black, they want an abortion. It's refreshing to meet someone who values life like you do."

I told him, "I had an abortion years ago, doctor, for different reasons—I was alone and terrified—I didn't have good advice—I didn't know what to do. But I will never do that again."

He seemed genuinely pleased about my decision, and his attitude restored my respect for the medical profession. It also made me realize what a hard line doctors must walk in our world today as they help people from so many different backgrounds and beliefs to make decisions they cannot dictate.

Our meeting with Dr. Johnson turned out to be even more encouraging because he told us a number of facts about our daughter that actually improved her chances. First, our child was female, which was good because males apparently suffer more with that disability. Second, her lungs and heart appeared to be strong. Third, her kidneys were developing normally. And finally, there were no facial disfigurements that he could detect. All of these things pointed to a best-case scenario.

Dr. Johnson at that point referred us to Dr. John Freeman, a world-renowned pediatric neurologist and chairman of the Pediatric Neurology Department at Johns Hopkins Hospital. He has written several award-winning books on epilepsy in children and also childhood neurological disorders. We arrived at the hospital totally intimidated, wanting to hear that the baby would be fine. I was uncomfortable, and the delivery was near; I was very stressed, drained and tired, close to becoming completely unnerved. For once, I knew I needed some real compassion, not just the "truth."

However, everything went wrong from the start. Our appointment had gotten lost, and we arrived unannounced and unexpected. They had to page Dr. Freeman, and when he arrived, he was clearly embarrassed about all the confusion. He's a striking man, over six feet tall, with receding, graying hair and a distinguished, almost intimidating aura. Often he comes across as brusque and to the point, though over time I would come to know him as a deeply compassionate and loving man whose brusqueness only serves to hide a genuine inner sensitivity for children and their parents.

However, in this situation he leaned back in his chair and spelled it all out in a very clinical, almost detached manner. He said, "She could be born perfectly fine, perfectly healthy. She could require the implantation of a shunt immediately following delivery. She could have a mild learning disability. Or she could be completely vegetative. Or she could die in the womb."

As he reached those last words and the full impact of what he was saying hit me, what strength I had left seemed to drain away as if a plug had been pulled, and I simply gazed at him in shock. I honestly thought we had heard the worst, and here he had painted a picture that exceeded even our own worst-case scenario.

Diana Pillas, Dr. Freeman's assistant and the coordinator-counselor for the Birth-Defects Clinic, had arrived late, but when she saw my reaction, she handed me some tissues. A pretty woman of Greek descent with curly blonde hair and piercing light green eyes, Diana has worked with Dr. Freeman for many years. She is literally his right hand and has even coauthored some of his books. She immediately began talking to me gently and lovingly. What she said I cannot remember, but her words and manner provided me the comfort and compassion I so desperately needed at that point. She reassured me, "We will do everything in our power to help your baby."

For several moments we explored our various options with Dr. Freeman, and he reiterated Diana's assurances that they would be available should we need them. As we left the office, Diana handed me one of her business cards, telling me, "This is my name and my business number." As I reached for it, she pulled it back, picked up a pen, and wrote on the back. She handed it back, saying, "This is my home phone number. If at any time you need to talk to someone about anything, please feel free to call me." I would learn later that she rarely, if ever, did this with patients, and here we had just met her for the first time.

*

Because the baby was diagnosed hydrocephalic, Dr. Ashai moved the delivery from Howard County General Hospital to Johns Hopkins Hospital where there was a state-of-the-art Neonatal Intensive Care Unit equipped to handle high-risk infant births. Dr. Ashai felt it was in the baby's best interest to deliver by cesarean section rather than to expose her to the trauma of a normal delivery through the birth canal. He also advised us that once her lungs were fully developed we could proceed with the delivery. We wondered how they would know the lungs were complete, and he said a weekly amniocentesis test would indicate when the baby's lungs were ready. I said with some trepidation, "Weekly?"

He replied, "Weekly."

✱

During that time, beyond the handicap issue, two significant problems played on my mind. I worried first about my abilities as a mother. "I'm not very child-oriented," I would often moan to Brian, for the thousandth time voicing a worry that had plagued me for years. I'm not very maternal and did not know how to relate to children.

"What if I don't like being a mother, Brian?"

He'd answer with a shake of his head, "Believe me, honey, you'll like it. And you'll be good at it. You're already the most obsessive housekeeper I ever met."

We'd both laugh and savor once more the thought of a little voice crying for our touch in the night, little feet scampering over the tiles, little eyes peering into a book as one of us read.

Repeatedly I knelt at my bed and told God that my vow hadn't changed. I would see this through no matter what.

All this time Brian and I clung to one another and tried to find some solace in the "grace of God" that we kept hearing about in our new church home, Chapelgate, where our pastor frequently referred to concepts like "God's sovereignty," His "goodness and grace," and the fact that "He always works all things together for good to those who love Him and are called by Him."

In many ways these were totally new ideas for both of us. We'd never heard them growing up, or even in the churches we'd attended previous to Chapelgate. We kept telling one another it would somehow "all work out" and we should cease worrying. But I guess I wasn't ready to believe that, and it was difficult to escape the constant fears and doubts that hounded us.

Meanwhile, friends and family rallied around us. I had six baby showers, and Brian's coworkers at the Holiday Inn in downtown Baltimore even gave him a seventh surprise shower. In fact, it was interesting for me to see Brian as the "star" for once. They sat him in a special chair, just like they did me at my showers, and they even forced Brian to wear the official "shower bonnet," an explosion of bows and ribbons that nicely set off his crimson face.

Our second problem was even more uplifting and not fraught at all with the kind of anxiety we were experiencing on other levels, and that was what we would name our little one. That brings up a unique tradition in my family that I've always found fascinating. Our daughter's first two names were already selected, actually before either Brian or I was born. My name, Alsie Lucille, is the same as my mother's name and her mother and then each mother all the way back for thirteen generations. Astonishing as it seems to me at times, I am literally "Alsie the Thirteenth." My name came from Alsace-Lorraine in France, where my family originated. Alsie the First was born sometime in the seventeenth century in France. Perhaps on a whim, or even a dare, Alsie Lucille the First decided to give her firstborn daughter the same name: Alsie Lucille Whatever the Second.

That started a family tradition. Thus, the name has been passed on through thirteen generations. I, Alsie Lucille "the Thirteenth" Kelley, knew long before I ever met Brian that our firstborn daughter must be named Alsie Lucille.

Thus, the issue for us was the baby's "pet" name, or the name by which she'd be called by family members. All the Alsies had nicknames that were used instead of the given name. My nickname is "Peanut," and my mother's is "PeeWee." (I should tell you, though, that only family members call us by those names, and in both my and my mother's case, should outsiders refer to us that way, watch out!) Brian and I decided to break with that element of the tradition, though, and give our baby a legal name she could properly use in school and everywhere else.

Both of us had seen the movie *Anastasia* late in the pregnancy about the youngest daughter of Czar Nicholas, who supposedly escaped execution during the Russian Revolution. It was a powerful story, and we were both deeply moved. Brian wanted, in particular, a name appropriate for a little girl, a name that would be both beautiful and special, perhaps even a little unusual. He suggested we name her Alsie Lucille "Anastasia" Kelley. We would call her Stasia for short.

I'm usually the one to initiate such things, but in this case I readily agreed. It came to have even deeper meaning for both of us when we later learned that Brian's grandfather's sister was named Anastasia and that the Greek word, which is used in the Bible, means "resurrection."

As my time to deliver drew near, we felt buoyed up on the prayers and loving encouragements of friends and church members. We were now in the eighth month of pregnancy, and Dr. Ashai informed us we needed to begin the amniocentesis testing to determine if Stasia's lungs were complete. I lived in some dread of this because back when the test was last performed, in my third month of pregnancy, it had been very uncomfortable. I was completely unprepared for the pain of the test now. By the time of the third scheduled amnio, the pain had reached an extreme, and I came down with the flu, coughing and hacking constantly. I knew I couldn't take anymore amnios. I was physically and emotionally exhausted, so I asked Dr. Ashai to schedule the cesarean, saying, "This child is in God's hands. Let's please go ahead with the delivery. I can't face another amnio."

Dr. Ashai planned the delivery for May 19. We left that dank, gray morning after a sleepless night and arrived at Johns Hopkins at 6:00 A.M. Months before, our church secretary, Pauline Chisholm, had asked me if there was anything Dr. Adams or she could do, and I had said, "If Dr. Adams could come and pray with us before the C-section, I would really appreciate this." I knew this was asking a lot, but I have always had a deep fear of hospitals. Pauline had promised that she was sure he would make every effort to get there before the operation. Astonishingly, Dr. Adams arrived moments before I was wheeled down to the operating room. The one thing that stands out in my memory was how he asked God to "give the doctors and nurses compassionate and gentle hands as they perform their various tasks with Stasia and Alsie." He had targeted precisely my need, and to this day I remember that as another of God's special blessings in my life.

Stasia was born at 9:30 A.M. May 19, 1987. She was about to be whisked to the Neonatal Intensive Care Unit, and only as they heard me whisper, "Can I see her?" did they hold her up for a brief moment before they rushed her away to the treatment room. As the doctors finished stitching up my hip-to-hip C-section and took me to the recovery room, Dr. Ashai visited the NICU to check on Stasia and then came back to Brian and me. I asked him, "Is she pretty?"

He said, "She's beautiful."

I smiled as if to say, That's what you're supposed to say, but is she really pretty?

As if understanding my expression, he grew very serious and said, "I don't tell all my mothers that their babies are beautiful. I really don't."

I was amazed as he reiterated, "She really is beautiful, Alsie."

Joy Sublime

THE FIRST TWO DAYS following the C-section I remained in my private room. I slipped in and out of a morphine-induced fog and slept, thinking of little more than relieving the pain. Brian stayed in the room with me at night and visited the baby during the day, bringing back glowing reports about Stasia when I was conscious enough to receive them. I was terrified of being alone, partly because of my hospital phobia, and partly because I felt so helpless in the face of the excruciating pain and therefore needed Brian to stay close by.

But beyond these fears was another anxiety, much deeper and in some ways more troublesome. My mother had burst into the recovery room, shouting, "They're torturing that little baby!"

I immediately asked what was happening.

"They have a rubber band on her forehead, and it's slipped down into her eye, and now it's stuck!" she yelled. "They're brutalizing her."

Next, the nurses brought by a picture of Stasia all bandaged and hooked up to a web of wires. She looked so vulnerable and defenseless that my immediate response was one of tenderness and a fierce need to protect her. But the haunting vision of Stasia suffering, horribly handicapped, and sliding towards death imprinted itself in my mind.

It all confirmed something I had feared ever since Dr. Freeman had told me Stasia might die in the womb. I was afraid to see her, to get attached to her, if it was all going to end in just a week or two.

Stasia was being treated in the Neonatal Intensive Care Unit at Johns Hopkins, the medical unit we soon learned to call the NICU. Although only two weeks premature, Stasia's doctors were adamant that her development was more like an eight-week pre-emie. She was less than half the size of Brian's arm, and he repeatedly encouraged me to "come and see." My fear mounted during those first two days as I debated where and when to see my baby. The nurses kept strategizing how to get me and the baby together so we could bond.

However, I kept delaying taking that step for the first two days. I gave Brian various reasonable excuses, but I knew the real issue for me was that once I picked up that little one, my life would never be the same again. Every hour Brian coaxed me, bringing back all kinds of scintillating reports—she was out of the oxygen tent, he'd held her hand, she looked out of danger. Finally, on the third evening, I sensed the moment had come: it was now or never; I had to turn this corner in my life. With a sigh of relief I said to Brian, "Take me down to the NICU."

Brian helped me into a wheelchair, and we slowly rolled into the NICU. The lights were low, and we were alone as he wheeled me to the front of the incubator. I looked at my sleeping baby, and Brian said, "Do you want to hold her?"

She was so small and delicate-looking, so I said, "Do you think it's okay?"

"I don't think there'll be a problem." He put her in my arms.

It was a moment so weighted with hope that my heart pounded as I took her. But then I turned to peer into the face of this tiny, angelic child, and as I looked into her eyes, something happened.

Doctors talk about a mother and child bonding and the special, almost "mystical" union that occurs. And that something happened to me in that moment. My hopes—my life—had been riding on this desire for so many years. And here the fourteenth Alsie Lucille was . . . in my arms. She was beautiful, soft, tender, tiny. Something inside me just billowed. It was a physical feeling of enlargement, a sensation of filling, as if my body suddenly could no longer contain my heart. This child was ours, our first, and God seemed to be blessing me with those first pangs of jubilation that all first mothers must feel. It was an entrancing moment, and I was overwhelmed with joy and every good emotion a mom can experience under such circumstances.

Stasia was the fourteenth "Alsie Lucille" in fourteen generations. She had deep blue eyes that seemed to say, when she looked directly at me or Brian, that she knew much more than she was letting on. Her hair was a rich golden blonde, with tiny tresses and a small cowlick. Weighing only four pounds, she had been two weeks premature, a tiny raindrop of a girl.

Amazingly, her head did not even appear to be enlarged or hydrocephalic. She looked normal and healthy, and she was *ours*. Instantly the pain of the past five months vanished, and I began to believe not only that all was well, but that she wasn't handicapped in any way at all. I whispered to her, now blinking back at me with her metallic blue eyes, "Whatever this is, we're going to beat it. We can win against this. I know it."

It was a fragrant, holy moment that became the second landmark in Brian's and my relationship. Nurses stood around us in hushed silence and congratulated Brian and me as I held Stasia.

From that point on, I was in that NICU every minute I was allowed, and then some. When I was released from the hospital after my recuperation, four days later, Brian drove me in each morning to see Stasia, and I stayed until 11 P.M. each night when Brian ushered me out in tears. In fact, Brian was so embarrassed by my behavior he told the nurses, "I really don't beat her . . . She just doesn't want to leave the baby." I cuddled Stasia, talked to her, introduced her to her first stuffed animal (a little white teddy bear), and played "Brahms' Lullaby" on a tiny pink quilted music box Rosemary Cerra, a coworker of Brian's and an honorary aunt, had bought for Stasia. I kissed her, fed her, rocked her for hours, and just held her and held her and held her. The joy couldn't be contained.

Both Brian and I were acutely aware of the care that was being given to Stasia in the NICU to get her weight up and to get her healthy enough to leave. Each day I politely asked about anything they'd discovered, trying very hard to suppress my own normal inclination to be assertive and direct. I did not want to upset anyone who was taking care of Stasia for fear that could have adverse results, even though I knew Johns Hopkins was one of the most prestigious and professional hospitals in the world. All the nurses and doctors I talked to were cordial and encouraging, obviously trying to allay my fears. But I honestly felt they were excessively secretive and noncommittal about what they had found, if anything. Their typical reply was, "It's inconclusive."

Deep down, I was still apprehensive that Stasia might die, and each time I held her in the NICU—for hours at a stretch, fourteen hours a day—I lived in fear of some doctor taking me or Brian aside and saying, "I'm sorry, but there's a serious problem."

Nonetheless, as Stasia and I bonded, I fell deeper in love with her. I determined that nothing would prevent me from being the best mother Stasia could possibly have. As we continued spending so many hours in the NICU, I also began forging friendships with other parents, the nurses and doctors, and even Stasia's roommates. Some of them weighed less than a pound, more gauze pads as diapers, and were dressed in Cabbage Patch doll clothing because it was the only kind that was small enough.

Stasia did not seem to be making normal progress, though, and the doctors would not allow us to take her home. She wasn't learning to suck. She wasn't responding well to stimuli. She wasn't gaining weight. Several of the doctors even believed she might be blind, and possibly deaf.

Daily tests marauded through our routine. Stasia was stuck with needles, put under the rays of various machines, probed and prodded, kneaded like a lump of dough to "make sure all was well." It was difficult for me to witness this, and although I knew it was for her and our best, I still didn't understand why so many tests had to be performed. Though there were obvious problems, in my mind she was a preemie. She looked normal to me, in fact healthier than many of the babies I saw in the NICU, some of whom were several months premature. Even though she still wasn't taking food by mouth—always through the NG (Nasogastric) Tube—I thought we could handle that, too.

Through it all, though, the doctors seemed to be maintaining a vow of silence about how much they would tell us.

By this time Stasia had been moved to a room the nurses called "the pasture." That was encouraging because it was a step up, but we still were not allowed to take her home. One day Brian and I faced one another over Stasia's bed. "What on earth is the problem?" I asked him. I was beginning to feel angry and frustrated. "Why aren't we allowed to take Stasia home?"

Brian answered, "Honey, the doctors know best, and they'll let us take her home when it's time."

That answer didn't satisfy me, and as time sprinted along, I fought harder to get a fix on the results of the tests. Always it was the same answer: "Inconclusive." Or, "Babies have to reach certain milestones, and we're looking for those developments."

To me, though, everyone continued to be inexplicably obscure. My woman's intuition told me they were hiding something. But I did not want to press too firmly about it, so I worked at being patient.

The seventh week finally hurried by. I was on the road every day at dawn from our home in Woodlawn and staying until Brian escorted me out at 11 P.M. I was tired of all the secretiveness, of all the "inconclusive" tests, of seeing my little Stasia in the sterile setting of a hospital NICU when she had a real home only minutes away.

Then there was a breakthrough: one of the nurses managed to get Stasia to take an ounce of formula by the mouth through a special Nuk nipple. This had been the one barrier that remained, and we were walking on air that finally Stasia was learning to eat by mouth.

I finally asked the head nurse and the doctor, "She's eating now. If the tests are inconclusive, why can't we take her home?"

They patiently repeated their standard answer: "Mrs. Kelley, please, we simply want to be sure she'll be all right. She's not sucking well, she's lethargic, and she's not responding to stimuli."

I countered, "But we know preemies are that way, and you taught us to use the NG tube to feed her. We can do that, so what's the point? You can do the tests whether she's here or at home!"

That night at home I had reached my limit. I told Brian as tears burned into my eyes, "I want to be a mother. I want to complain about night feedings and waking up at all hours. I want to wake up to her first cries. I want her to have a home! I want her to have a place that is hers, surrounded by her family—a home—a real home!"

Finally, after the seventh week, the doctors allowed us to stay the weekend with her alone. We stayed in a tiny room off the NICU. All night long the service elevators unloaded people and machines, and we got very little sleep. It was like trying to fall into a dead sleep in the middle of Grand Central Station. We were also terrified of making a mistake with Stasia's care that might delay her going home. However, when they saw we handled it fairly well, they relented and actually let us go home a day early.

We took Stasia home to our little yellow and blue nursery with every childish dream realized in living color. We wanted to give her the best of everything. Stuffed animals—a brown bear cub, a yellow duck, a white rabbit, and many others—lined the walls around the crib. Mobiles with colorful stuffed animals hung from the ceiling. A special wallpaper border with little angels and clouds hung on three walls. The fourth wall was papered in soft pastels, with letters of the alphabet and appropriate animals to go with each letter. I envisioned that as I changed her I would teach her the letters of the alphabet.

In many ways, things could not have been better for us from a psychological and spiritual standpoint. We felt blessed, assured, happy. Through our church a legion of friends and acquaintances provided full-course meals every single day of the seven weeks Stasia was in the NICU, even going so far as leaving a personalized note with each delivery. We were surrounded by loving, caring people who began calling, sending cards, and continuing to bring meals or just dropping by to play games and visit. I began to perceive the body of Christ in our church as an incredible life-support system, and I sensed that God was loving us through His people. We were both deeply impressed, in fact astonished. Our marriage had survived the emotional battering of the last few months, and we believed, above all, that if Stasia had any handicap, it could be overcome, we would see it through. Though we were too exhausted to think about the normal activities of a young married couple, a great joy percolated through our consciousness. Everything I had hoped and prayed for appeared to be coming to pass.

Thus, we came home with high hopes. Stasia shimmied around in the crib like any normal newborn. She responded to touch, to smells, to sounds. One of our first nights home she slept soundly all through the night. It was so startling that both of us awoke with a start when we realized all was quiet, and we bolted into the nursery, terrified that something had gone wrong. The monitor that kept watch over her heartbeat and breathing had not peeped, though, and we both peered over the edge of the crib into that angelic little face, wondering what on earth was going on.

"Is she breathing?" I finally whispered.

"I think so," Brian answered.

"Should we wake her?"

"I don't know."

"Is she all right?"

"I'm not sure."

"Maybe we should call the doctor."

"Maybe."

Then Stasia stirred, opened her eyes, and seemed to look at us and say, "Hey, what's up, kids?" We both laughed. This baby was going to be fine. Surely there was no great handicap. In fact, this was fun!

★

One of my greatest early experiences came in the form of a serendipitous feeling I noticed as I began the routine of taking care of our newborn. My greatest fear before the birth—besides all the dire warnings about hydrocephalus—was that I wouldn't know how to be a mother, that I'd be unable to communicate with my child, totally unable to relate to her. Although Stasia slept through the night mentioned above, that was the only time it ever happened. Normally I was up every two hours.

But one day as my mother sat reading in the family room, I hauled out the laundry and began folding Stasia's tiny white socks and shirts. Soon I was giggling happily, despite having had only about an hour of sleep in the last forty-eight hours. My mother looked up finally and said, "What on earth are you laughing about?"

I giggled again. "I don't know. It's the darnedest thing. I really like this."

"What do you mean, 'this'?"

"'This!' All of it. I like it. No, I love it."

"What do you mean, 'this'?" Mom insisted.

"The whole thing—getting up every other hour, changing her diapers, folding her laundry. I love being a mother!"

My mom just laughed. "You haven't had enough sleep. Perhaps you should go lie down."

"No, Mom," I said, enjoying the pangs of joy that seemed to infuse me, "it's this, this very thing I'm doing right now with the laundry . . . I love matching up the teeny-weeny little socks, folding the little shirts and pants, feeding her. She wakes up two, four, six times a night. Some nights I'm so exhausted, I just don't think I can get up one more time. But then I get up, walk into her room, look into that angelic face, and she's there in the crib, eyes open, looking at me like I'm the most important person on earth. I change her diapers, and I love it! It's the darnedest thing. Every trace of exhaustion . . . it all goes when I see her. She's so cute. I pick her up and hold her, and we talk and talk and talk. It's . . . Mom, I don't know what it is, but I just love it!"

I thought about it all again as I stared at my incredulous mother who didn't seem to understand what I was feeling. "I love doing her laundry. I love hearing her cry and wanting to be fed. You know, Mom, I'm not one of those women who gurgle and coo over children. But I sit in the rocker holding her, and all I can do is say, 'Thank You, God. Thank You for Stasia. Thank You for the doctors. Thank You for our home, and for the love and care the doctors have shown us, and for leading us to Johns Hopkins, and for Chapelgate, and for this perfect little human being.' I go on and on, just thanking God. It's totally amazing. I don't know what else to say."

Mom went back to her reading, perhaps a little amazed at this profuse demonstration of motherly bliss, but that was how I felt.

It was a fantastic and thrilling spiritual high. The thing I'd dreamed about for years had come to pass. And I was not stymied, not overwhelmed, not broken by it. It had become the defining experience of my life.

The Bomb Drops

THE WEEKEND STASIA CAME HOME, another very different sort of tragedy struck. Miss Ollie, my blonde cocker spaniel whom I'd had since my college days, suffered congestive heart failure. Even as Brian and I tried to make the newest member of our household comfortable and happy, we fought a losing battle to save Miss Ollie. We took her to the vet that weekend, and he administered some medication that gave her the rest she needed. After spending a weekend in the hospital she came home, apparently well.

A few days later she began suffering from incontinence. She wouldn't eat, and what she did eat didn't stay down. She lay on the cool bathroom floor, sucking air in long, ragged breaths.

With my mother watching Stasia, Brian and I took Miss Ollie on that terrible journey back to the vet, telling him she was in extreme pain and near death. He advised us he could prescribe medication to ease her suffering, but he believed putting the suffering dog to sleep was the wisest and most compassionate course.

Miss Ollie had been with me for over fourteen years. It was another one of those decisions that rake at your insides like barbed-wire. Both Brian and I knew we could not let her suffer with no hope of recovery. After several minutes of thought and prayer, we agreed to let Miss Ollie be put to sleep.

Somehow we muddled through and turned our new grief
around by drinking in the strange and new thrill of having our first
child in our home. Alsie Lucille the Fourteenth.

I began noticing little things about Stasia I'd never known or
heard of before about babies, though I'm sure every mother goes
through the same experiences. One of the great events of our day
was showing Stasia some new thing about life in this world. She
wasn't very sensitive to light—several of the doctors believed she
might be blind—but touch, sound, and anything caressing her skin
provoked a strong reaction.

One summer afternoon Brian and I took Stasia for a walk as we
searched out model homes in view of a possible move to Columbia,
Maryland. Because the doctors thought Stasia would be particularly susceptible to colds and illnesses, I had to be far more careful
in taking her anywhere. This was one of our first jaunts into the
outside world together.

I walked along, and a gentle breeze came up, sweeping over us
and caressing Stasia's face. As I watched, Stasia's face lit up, her
arms lifted elegantly as if trying to fly, and an expression of wonder spread across her face as if she were saying to herself, "This is
new!" Her eyes were big and wide, her mouth pursed.

Laughing, we again drank in the wonder of life and its newness.
Through our daughter we were experiencing the joy and thrill of
discovery all over again. And again the conviction throbbed
through me that nothing could ruin this. Stasia would be the highlight of our lives; whatever problems arrived, we would beat them
together.

Above all, nothing appeared to me or Brian to be wrong with
Stasia. She continued to move around in the crib and would even
lift her head up while on her stomach, craning to see something
outside. I was sure she was exhibiting normal development, even
though I avoided reading any baby books for fear I might notice
something abnormal.

Then over the next month—through July 1987—something

changed. Stasia began crying steadily. She appeared terrified, and possibly in pain. She wouldn't eat and wasn't gaining weight. The only way we could get her to go to sleep was by placing a pacifier in her mouth. She would sleep until the pacifier slipped out. We worked out a multitude of ways of keeping the pacifier in, including literally "plugging the dike" like the little Dutch boy by watching her all night. We also had a little stuffed toy turtle whose head and neck were in perfect alignment with Stasia's mouth as she lay on her side in the crib. It would take me all night just to get Stasia to catnap, because she never really did sleep at that point.

In the early morning Brian would wake up and take over, giving me a couple hours in bed before the day began. He'd turn off the baby monitor, knowing I would be up at any sound. I would inevitably find him lying on the floor beside the crib with a pillow tucked under his head. Whenever Stasia cried, he'd reach up and "replug" the pacifier, and she'd catnap again.

Nonetheless, deep down I felt I was failing as a mother because the sleepless nights were getting worse and I could seem to do nothing to calm her. At still only five pounds, Stasia remained in great danger of the devastation of any illness, even a minor cold. It took me three hours to get her to take two ounces of formula.

As the crying continued, we visited the emergency room repeatedly. One day the doctors told us Stasia had a double hernia, but they couldn't operate because she was too small. Perhaps in a few months they'd be able to perform the surgery, but not yet.

Over a period of time Stasia would sleep only when she was held. Brian and I began taking turns on alternate nights, holding her in the family room from 12 P.M. to 6 A.M. Brian kept his humor, watching old movies on one of the cable channels. Frequently when I greeted him in the morning, exhausted but ready for my shift, I'd ask him how things were. He'd say, "Bogie and the Duke were tremendous. Gable was so-so."

It was wearing. We had an appointment in August to see a pediatric neurologist. We requested to see Dr. John Freeman, Chief of

Pediatric Neurology at Johns Hopkins, whom we'd consulted with briefly during my pregnancy and his assistant, Diana Pillas. We knew Dr. Freeman saw a multitude of young patients with every kind of neurological disorder imaginable. We considered it a real blessing from God that he agreed to see us. Though it was still unclear what handicaps Stasia might have, we planned to discuss the problems we were seeing when we went for the appointment.

I had already come to see Dr. Freeman as a man with a depth of love and sensitivity not always apparent in his sometimes direct manner. I soon discovered he is as likely to quote from Winnie the Pooh as the Book of Job, and he fills his conversation with a dry wit wedded to genuine compassion. From our first meeting I was drawn to him as the only doctor for Stasia.

During our appointment Dr. Freeman led us into the Pediatric Neurology Clinic with Diana Pillas and a group of "learning" doctors and performed a battery of tests, including using a tiny rubber hammer to test Stasia's reflexes and a multitude of other items. Finally he turned out all the lights in the room. He then turned on a single lamp and set it beside Stasia's temple. To me it was an incredible sight. My little girl's head brightened as if a light bulb had been switched on inside of it. I said, "Oh, how pretty."

But the room around me was ominously quiet. In the back of my mind I realized that brain matter inside someone's head should be dense, not translucent as Stasia's was. But Brian and I just waited to hear what Dr. Freeman would say.

Moments later Dr. Freeman briefly left the room. Later Diana told me he was visibly shaken by what he had seen. I did not know this until years later; at the time I was only concerned that Dr. Freeman might allow one of the residents to handle our case instead of taking it himself.

Dr. Freeman returned, though, asked if there were any other problems, and offered to answer any questions. Since we had none, he simply had us schedule another appointment and told us to stay in touch. We left hopeful, figuring that no news is good news, and went home pleased that we'd gotten to see him.

With our hopes rejuvenated by the meeting with Dr. Freeman, we concentrated our effort on helping Stasia eat and gain weight so the hernia operation could take place. However, it became a vicious cycle: Stasia would not eat because of the pain, and she could not have the hernia operation because she wasn't gaining weight. The doctor was adamant that we could not go ahead with the operation without risking her life. However, it soon became obvious that she was steadily deteriorating because of the pain and the lack of food. After much discussion, we finally persuaded the pediatric surgeon to schedule the operation for September even if Stasia did not gain the required weight.

It was during this period, when Stasia passed the four-month mark, that she began performing what we initially called her "aerobic workouts." As I held her, Stasia's eyes would suddenly shift sharply to the left and lock. In slow motion, she raised both arms and abruptly jackknifed. She did this two or three times, then would stop as abruptly as she had started. It began as an occasional occurrence. Then it happened weekly. Soon it was once a day. In time it would reach twenty to thirty times a day during all hours.

We arrived in September for the operation. The doctors examined her and discovered she was dehydrated. I said, "Of course she's dehydrated—she won't eat!"

They put her on an IV right away and admitted her to an isolation room. That same day we had the follow-up appointment with Dr. Freeman. We wheeled Stasia down in her baby carriage with the portable IV beside her.

Dr. Freeman immediately asked us about Stasia's being on the IV, and we explained about the hernia operation. Then he asked us how things were going with the baby. I casually mentioned Stasia's "workouts." Dr. Freeman's handsome, suntanned face showed no emotion. He questioned me closely about it, and I said, "It's almost like she's playing. Her eyes move to the side and lock, then she jackknifes. It started once a week, but now it occurs once or twice a day."

Neither Brian nor I had any idea anything serious might be wrong. We'd never seen behavior like this, but otherwise Stasia still seemed to us to be normal. In the process we also mentioned about having to get up and feed and comfort Stasia nearly every hour of the night. Shock registered on Dr. Freeman's face, and I said, "Well, that's normal for newborns, isn't it?"

He answered, "Not for five-month-old babies. She should not be waking up every hour." He suggested we might try using chloral hydrate to sedate her and help her get a full night's sleep.

Instantly I was alarmed. "Sedate a baby?" This was my first inkling that something serious might indeed be wrong. No one we'd ever known had sedated their baby.

"It's the only way you'll get a full night's sleep. You can't keep functioning on this level."

He wrote out a prescription, and I asked him again about the "workouts." He said, "It could be seizures, but let's not worry about that until the hernia operation is out of the way. After the operation, we'll transfer her to my floor, and then we'll figure this out."

When we went back upstairs, a nurse asked how it had gone with Dr. Freeman, and I mentioned he had said Stasia might be having seizures. She left without revealing a hint of concern, and a moment later the surgeon and another doctor returned to question us. After hearing our answers, they told us they would delay the operation because of the seizures. I said, "Doctor, this child is going to die if you don't operate." I told him what Dr. Freeman had said. He told me, "You should not put a person under anesthesia when they're having seizures." He refused to go through with the operation and left the room.

We were stunned and deeply disappointed, but after a few minutes' discussion I decided to call Dr. Freeman. We had to get Stasia through this!

Dr. Freeman wasn't available until midnight. But when we

finally spoke, he promised to straighten out the problem. The next morning the doctor performed the operation. After a recovery of three days, Stasia had come through with flying colors, and we were greatly elated.

At that point Dr. Freeman moved her down to Pediatric Neurology and ordered a CAT scan and other tests. The doctors were also monitoring her "workouts," which Dr. Freeman now referred to as "infantile spasms." The following evening, Stasia underwent the CAT scan. We watched as her tiny form was swallowed up by this immense machine. The operators led Brian and me both to a side room where we watched a computer screen that showed us what the machine was seeing. It was as if we were standing above Stasia and looking down on the top of her head. Where the screen should have pictured Stasia's brain we saw nothing but white space with a thin, black line along the perimeter of the skull, just like a typical negative photograph. Again I sensed that her brain should have been dense, perhaps black, and that made both of us apprehensive.

The next day when the tests were completed, Dr. Freeman arrived while I was holding Stasia in her room, and he said, "Put the baby down on the bed, Alsie, we need to talk."

I immediately replied, "It's no problem. I can talk with her in my arms."

He said again, "Put the baby down. We need to go into the conference room."

"Well, I can take her with me."

We had a momentary tug-of-wills, and finally I acquiesced, sensing the gravity of whatever was on his mind. He led us into the floor conference room. I sat stiffly in the chair, a sinking feeling inside me. Several other residents were there, and also Maybian Gloth, who was Stasia's "primary nurse." I steeled myself for what the doctor was about to say.

He finally spoke. "Brian, Alsie, what the CAT scan reveals is that Stasia has suffered tremendous brain damage. She has only the lining of a brain—really only a smattering here and there."

Then he sat quietly and waited. I looked at Brian, and he returned my strained gaze. Strangely, I felt nothing. I was in absolute shock, numb, the way I'd felt at times when learning of a loved one's passing. At the same time I found myself waiting for someone to laugh and say it was all a joke.

But no one spoke.

When I finally grasped what Dr. Freeman was saying, after another long silence, I said, "What do you mean, she only has the lining of a brain?"

"Basically it means she may sit up on her own, she may say a few words, she may even be able to take a few steps, but that's about the most you can expect."

My heart was hammering now, and I glanced at Brian. He gazed evenly at Dr. Freeman, taking it all in as he usually did, not speaking until he was ready. I was still frozen in place, trying to work through the bubbling confusion in my mind. Dr. Freeman remained silent, as if waiting for what he'd said to register.

It was as if I couldn't think anymore, and the next question that came out was, "What about life expectancy?"

"She could have a normal life span," Dr. Freeman said immediately, "if we can stop the infantile spasms. We'll put her on prednisone to stop them. Either they'll stop or they'll be replaced by adult seizures. At this point we should hope that they just stop and she goes on without them."

Both Brian and I sat there stone-still, in abject silence. I didn't know what more to ask or say. A mixture of anguish and rage flared on the edge of my consciousness, but I was still too numb to go on. I knew I needed time to think and time to pray. I was aware of people talking around me and Dr. Freeman asking more questions, but I didn't seem to hear anything until he asked me, what seemed an eternity later, "What are you feeling, Alsie?"

I gazed out the window before answering. Deep within me I felt a violent internal heat, something I can only describe as rage. Finally I turned to him and said quietly, "Angry . . . I feel so angry."

Dr. Freeman's eyes didn't leave my face. There was another long pause until I said, "I'm just so angry. I wish I could hit somebody."

He said gently, "You can hit me if it will make you feel better."

I knew he meant it. I sensed he was struggling to comfort me. I slowly turned away from the window and said, "I don't want to hit you. You're the only one who can help us."

There was more discussion, and finally he walked with us back to Stasia's room and said, "We'll talk again tomorrow."

Moments later Brian and I stood over Stasia's crib and peered at our little one sleeping quietly, her light hair framing the angelic, composed face. Tears filled my eyes, and I bent down and kissed her. "I love you, sweetheart. Mama loves her little angel."

When I stood, Brian's eyes met mine. Instantly we came together in a fierce hug, both sobbing. "What are you feeling?" I finally asked. I could feel his body trembling against mine.

"Scared . . . Real scared."

We held one another for a long time, trying to work through the terrible words that had just shattered our joyous, peaceful little world. Brian told me later he felt broken inside, a father who was suddenly rendered useless and impotent. He'd been brought up to believe in principles like "a father fixes things that get broken," "A father protects his little ones," "A father bandages cuts and scrapes and wipes away tears." But how could he be a father to our little girl? How could he protect her from this?

As the sobbing ended, I felt numb and drained. We parted and sank into two different chairs, saying nothing to one another, staring into space. I was aware of a great silence around me as all the floor personnel worked together to meet our need for solitude.

I remember sitting there struggling to make some sense of Dr. Freeman's words but ending up feeling isolated and abandoned by God.

Dr. Adams

ASHORT TIME LATER our pastor, Dr. Lane Adams, called, as if he had some advance warning of what was happening. When I picked up the phone, his concerned baritone voice said, "How are you, Alsie?"

I answered tightly, still fighting the waves of anger inside, "Not very good."

After a few minutes of talk about the baby's condition, he said, "This is a difficult time, but, Alsie . . . I want to say something that might sound a little trite, but I believe it is true, and it conveys a powerful spiritual message. It's this: this circumstance will either make you bitter or it will make you better. Please don't misunderstand my intent, but I really believe God can use this situation for good in your life, and also in Brian's and Stasia's."

I couldn't hold it in any longer. "Dr. Adams, I am angrier than I have ever been in my entire life. I cannot believe God could do this. This has destroyed my concept of a loving God. He couldn't do this to a child. This is sick. If I weren't so angry, I'd laugh. Nothing could be constructed more perfectly to give us everything we dreamed of and then take it all away inch by inch. I have to congratulate the devil. This is so diabolical—to take my firstborn and turn her brain to mush!"

Dr. Adams waited, and in the silence I launched into another angry tirade. When I finished, he said, "Alsie, what you're express-ing is completely normal, and I would even say Scriptural, consid-ering what you're facing. But I know God cares, and He understands the pain you're feeling."

"Where does it say that?"

"Jesus wept when He saw Martha's pain, Alsie, after the death of Lazarus."

"If God understands how I feel, why would He allow pain this deep, this raw in a person's life?"

"I suspect God's just waiting for His little girl to run out of steam."

"Why would He be waiting for that?"

"So He can walk with you through it. You can't see it until He takes you through it."

"Well, you don't know how much steam this little girl has."

He waited again, and then spoke softly as if thinking out loud but trying to choose his words cautiously. "Alsie, suppose when all is said and done, one day you could look back on it all and see this as the single most important experience of your life—would that make it worth it?"

It seemed that hours passed as I mulled this monumental absur-dity over in my mind, alternately accepting and rejecting it. On the one hand it sounded fine in theory, but I was in the middle of it, and it looked far from the "single most important event of my life." It looked far more like the "single greatest disaster of my life." In total disbelief and with great bitterness and anger I hissed, "That would be a bigger miracle than healing her!" But I understood something of what he was saying. I'd heard him preach on it. I'd read it at times in the Bible when I had my devotions. Somewhere deep inside I think I even knew it might be a truth I'd have to reckon with someday. Finally, very slowly I said, "Yes, I guess it would." I paused for only a microsecond, then added, "This is what I've always feared, Dr. Adams . . . All my life . . . I don't know how we can do this. I can't watch her die inch by inch."

"God will give you the strength, Alsie."

"God—who is He?" My voice was tinged with harsh sarcasm and bitterness. Even though I knew Dr. Adams was trying to be kind and understanding, I didn't want kindness—I wanted my baby to be well, to be healthy, to be normal.

"Alsie, you're angry and confused and very upset. No person could face what you're facing and not experience all those feelings."

I nodded with some agreement, leaning against the wall and trying to compose myself. "I don't know how I can make it through this, Dr. Adams. I just don't think I can face it. I thought I'd have enough of a challenge with a normal child. But this . . ."

He answered gently one more time, "God is there, Alsie. When you're ready, go to Him and talk about it. Meanwhile, I'm here, my wife Annette is here, your doctors are here. We'll all be there for you and will do the best we can to help. You're a strong girl. This isn't going to cripple you like you think; if I'm right in my theology, it will most assuredly strengthen you."

"I don't see how."

"One day you will. But don't worry about that now. Just hold on tight, and don't give up. I'll be coming over to the hospital later this week to see you, and we'll pray together."

"Okay." My throat and heart felt ragged, numb. Dr. Adams's quiet confidence was reassuring, but at that point only slightly. When he hung up, I felt cold and dead inside and began walking back to the room with feet of lead. How could I face this? How does anyone face it?

Once more the anger flared inside me and, closing my eyes, I said, half in prayer, half in accusing rage, "How could You do this to us?"

Of course, there was no answer. There was only the silence of hospital halls, the quietness of people walking by, headed to visit and try to comfort their relatives, friends, children. It all seemed so unfair, so unjust.

When I reached the room I stood at Stasia's bed. Gazing at that vulnerable and so very precious baby lying there so calm and reposed made Dr. Freeman's words seem all the more impossible. Her head was finely, almost perfectly shaped. The silky blonde tresses looked radiant and infinitely soft under the lights. How could a beautiful child like this have hardly any brain? How could God do this to us, to anyone?

I walked over to the window, looked up, and suddenly raised my fist and said vehemently in a coarse whisper, "I will *not* benefit from this!"

Only Ten Percent

NEWS OF OUR CALAMITY SPREAD through the unit. We would learn that in situations like ours, Dr. Freeman instructs all the personnel on his unit to be sensitized to the parents' feelings and anything they might say. In our case, he "dropped" the bomb at the beginning of the week, knowing we would be staying for the following several days as our daughter was monitored. We would discover that Dr. Freeman carefully chooses when and how he reveals devastating information so that he and his staff can offer the greatest support and counsel to the parents. That would become one of the traits which magnified our respect for him and his staff.

As a result, everyone around us initiated a special effort to draw out gently and kindly any feelings we might have. Once or twice a day Dr. Freeman would stop in, sit down, make himself comfortable as if he had all the time in the world, and talk, answer questions, and help us edge a micrometer closer to acceptance of our situation. He seemed to see himself not just as our baby's neurologist, but as a friend who wanted to help us work this through, knowing it would take hours and hours of thought, therapy, encouragement, and understanding. This was totally beyond the call of duty, and despite our internal pain Brian and I were both astonished. He often told us later that his philosophy of medicine was to "treat the entire family," knowing that an illness in a family affects everyone.

Only over the next few days did we begin to grasp the extent of Stasia's condition. One morning I asked, "What do you mean, Stasia only has the lining of her brain?"

Dr. Freeman said, "She is not hydrocephalic as we originally thought, but she is 'hydro-anencephalic,' which literally means, 'water and nothing else in the brain cavity.' It only happens about once in every fifteen hundred births. I see children like this maybe once every two years. It's very rare, but in plain terms, because of the brain damage she only has about 10 percent of a normal brain."

I said slowly, "What could possibly have caused this?"

"We know of only three things that can cause this kind of wholesale destruction of brain tissue: a tremendous drop in blood pressure, a series of strokes, or a viral infection. Our best guess is that it was a viral infection."

"But that's not possible. I was perfectly healthy throughout the entire pregnancy."

He answered, "Alsie, you have an adult immune system. Thousands of viruses pass in and out of your body all the time. You don't even know they're there until you develop a sore throat, a rash, a fever, whatever. In the first three months after conception, a baby is most vulnerable. A viral infection at that stage can literally wipe out a child's entire brain."

Instantly a thought occurred to me. I asked him, "Could an antibiotic do this to a child's brain?"

"What do you mean?"

I told him about the infection I'd had before I knew I was pregnant. The doctor had prescribed an antibiotic in that first month. Once I discovered I was pregnant, I immediately called the doctor and stopped it. Dr. Ashai assured me later when I asked him about it that nothing I had taken and nothing I had done had caused this problem. In fact, Dr. Ashai, who has a handicapped child himself, had earlier said to me, "Alsie, God sends these kinds of things as a test." It had reassured me at the time, but now those feelings of guilt were back in my mind.

Dr. Freeman reemphasized what Dr. Ashai had said. "Nothing you took and nothing you did could have caused this, Alsie. We've done multiple studies on this kind of problem, and we have found no common factor." He would tell us later that it was this very kind of guilt that often plagued the parents of handicapped children and wrecked their marriages. The search for answers continues in some parents for a lifetime.

For me, it would continue to be a nagging worry in the back of my mind, and though I later would come to different conclusions, I still struggle at times with that guilt, despite the assurances of so many different doctors.

Moments later I said, "It's my understanding we only use 10 percent of our brains anyway."

"Ten percent of a whole brain, Alsie. And her 10 percent is extremely damaged."

I was still too upset to sort it all through, but another thought struck me. I had recently read stories that Johns Hopkins and Dr. Freeman had pioneered something called a "hemispherectomy." In certain cases in which disease attacked a child's brain, it is possible to remove the diseased half, and eventually the remaining half takes over the functions of the whole. I asked Dr. Freeman about that.

"That only works when you still have half a good brain, Alsie. We don't even have half here. It's just the lining, nothing else."

"But surely you can do something, Dr. Freeman. Can't you fix this?"

The august doctor gazed at me as kindly as I think a man can and said, "Alsie, your daughter has just enough of a brain to survive, just enough to keep the basic functions—heart and lungs—going."

Brian gripped my hand. I fought back another surge of tears, and after more words of encouragement the doctor ended the meeting by saying, "We'll take this one step at a time, Alsie. Let's just see what happens with what we're doing now."

At the end of the week Stasia was released from the hospital, and we went back home to Woodlawn with a deep sense of betrayal and bitterness. I felt as if I had died and we were only going home to wait for the burial.

Annette and Suzy

S HORTLY AFTER WE SETTLED BACK in at home, Annette Adams, the pastor's wife, called and invited me to have lunch with her and her married daughter, Suzy. I was amazed that she would invite a woman who had been so caustic to her husband, but I quickly accepted, feeling desperately lonely and grateful for an opportunity for a little companionship. I looked forward to being pampered for an hour or so and to talk about something frivolous and perhaps humorous. Deep down, though, I wondered if Annette might also offer some insight into God's character that might explain the things I was feeling.

One of the problems that was bothering me was how so many people seemed to regard handicapped children, and, by implication, my daughter. Doctors had offered abortion. Nearly everyone I knew expressed some measure of horror or pity—not sympathy but pity about the fact that I would have to live with this all my life. In many cases they seemed to run from it as if Stasia's neurological damage were contagious. One friend had even asked her own doctor what he would counsel me, and he had said, "I'd get rid of it." Several had suggested we put Stasia in an institution. I loved Stasia and regarded her as a precious blessing from God, and it grieved me that no one seemed to see any value in her life whatsoever.

Annette had prepared a lovely meal, and we made small talk, gradually moving to the subject of my own anger and my feeling abandoned and unloved by God. As Suzy and Annette both listened to me ventilate my feelings, Annette became very serious and said, "Alsie, you need to know that your child, Stasia, has great worth in the eyes of God. She is not worthless, not useless. He loves her as much as He loves any of us, but more than that, she is significant in His eyes. She matters to Him, Alsie, and she has real worth."

She read several texts from the Bible about how God "knit us together" in the womb and how He personally "fashioned" us with His own hands. She reiterated, "Believe me, Alsie, God values Stasia as much as anyone of great and high achievements, and she has great stature in His eyes, regardless of her handicaps."

Annette's words surprised me to the point of tears. For a moment I could not speak, but then I quickly regained my composure, and Annette said something else.

"The other thing I want to share with you, Alsie, is that there is nothing that could ever separate you from the love of God."

I was absolutely stunned. My background was imbued with the experience of, "If you're good, good things will happen to you; if you're bad, all of that is withdrawn and you're isolated, rejected, ignored. You don't even exist." As an adult, I translated that childhood belief into the idea that if God is sovereign and this terrible thing has happened, what did I do wrong? Why does God no longer love me?

I said to Annette, "Nothing?"

She said, "That's right. Absolutely nothing."

This was a concept that had been for me unheard, unknown, and unfelt. Today I'd call it unconditional love. At that moment it was so powerful, so new, so different, I could barely speak. I asked her, "Where does it say that?"

She recited verses from Romans 8: "I am convinced that neither death nor life, nor angels, nor principalities, nor things present, nor things to come, nor powers, nor height nor depth, nor any other created thing, can separate us from the love of God in Christ Jesus." Annette said again, "Nothing can separate you from Him, Alsie, and He most assuredly did not allow this to happen to you to hurt you."

I listened to her intently, again surprised and stunned by her earnestness. She had zeroed in precisely on what I needed to hear. Strangely, that week when I had come home, Brian and I were tired, having had little sleep, Stasia was crying, and something inside me snapped. I ran upstairs, slammed the bedroom door, sat down on my bed, threw my fist at Heaven, and shouted, "I hate You, God. I hate Your Heaven, I hate Your Hell, I hate Your angels, I hate Your devils. I hate this whole thing." And then I sat there waiting for God to do something. I fully expected that Brian would find a cinder in the middle of the bed.

All that was instantly in my mind as Annette now said, "Nothing can separate you from the love of God." But I said in a slightly patronizing way, "Oh, there is one thing that could separate me from God, Annette, and that is my temper. You've never seen it, but believe me it's awesome."

Annette asked, "Have you ever read the Psalms?"

"No."

"Well, you should read them. David frequently showed real anger to God in many of the Psalms. And it never separated him from God."

Again I was amazed. I asked other questions, and as we began talking more about Stasia and how much I appreciated having this opportunity to talk with other women and get away from the hectic pace at home, Suzy offered, "If you ever need someone to babysit for Stasia so you can get out or run errands or go to a luncheon or something, please call me."

Again I was so surprised, I didn't know how to answer. No one had ever offered that with Stasia. People were terrified of her. They didn't even offer to hold her. I said, "Why would you want to do that, Suzy?"

She answered, "It would be a real privilege for me to have a chance to care for her and be with her." In my mind I suddenly realized Suzy was reinforcing Annette's words of only minutes before. They were the first two people outside of the hospital to say Stasia had real worth and value as a human being in the eyes of God and others. Those simple words from Annette and Suzy touched me deeply and stuck with me through the pain of the next year. It was another one of those moments that today I can look back to and see that even then God was pouring upon us His love and grace.

Every Two Weeks

THE PRIMARY PROBLEM at this point, in Dr. Freeman's mind, was that of controlling Stasia's infantile spasms. He prescribed prednisone, a strong steroid that a patient can only use for a limited time. It carries such side effects as crankiness, water retention, increased appetite, and rashes and acne on the face. Stasia was actually hungry! She'd be on the sofa, smacking her lips and eager for the bottle. She ate like a mother's dream for the first time in her life. In some ways it seemed like the most normal period of our household. She was literally a butterball. And for a while the seizures slowed down.

But by December the doctors had to begin weaning her off the medication. Immediately the seizures returned, with increasing frequency.

We were seeing Dr. Freeman and Diana Pillas every two weeks. The sessions were often an hour or two, sometimes as many as three hours straight. Dr. Freeman usually scheduled us as the last appointment in the day, so we could go on for as long as needed. In fact, we often wondered why on earth they were spending so much time with us. Frequently his examination of Stasia seemed almost cursory, although it was always thorough. Brian and I would arrive at the meeting armed with a list of questions, determined not to let them change the focus of the session to information about us. But Dr. Freeman and Diana would always cleverly turn the conversation around to our home life, our involvement in church, our interpersonal communication, and especially my need for interests other than caring for the baby. They especially zeroed in on me, often asking me questions such as, "How are you doing, Alsie?," to which I'd answer in cheery voice, "Fine. Just great." Then they'd probe a little deeper and inevitably unearth the truth. Or if they didn't get it to their satisfaction, they'd simply look at Brian, who'd give an immediate thumbs down and negate every chirpy thing I'd just said.

It became the wonder of our life that they were spending so much time with us. And finally we began to realize that they believed in us, they wanted our marriage to hold together, and above all, they wanted us to succeed as a couple in the midst of our tragedy. They told us once that 80 to 90 percent of marriages break up when they bring a child into the world with handicaps like Stasia's. As I mulled that statistic over in my mind, we both realized they were committed to helping us survive intact—no, more than intact—to survive with perhaps an even better marriage as the result of what we'd gone through.

On one particular visit Dr. Freeman plunged right into the personal questions and encouragements for an hour or so. When he finally stood up to leave, I suddenly said, "Dr. Freeman, aren't you going to examine Stasia?"

He turned and answered with a mischievous smile, "Oh, she's fine. It's you two I'm worried about."

Looking back, I realize now that he knew there was not much he could do to cure Stasia's condition, but our marriage was another matter. We appreciated how much time he was spending with us, but we did not realize how extraordinary his and Diana's efforts were on our behalf until one day we met another parent in the waiting room of the Clinic. A man sitting across from us asked us about Stasia and then who our doctor was. I told him, and he began a story about his daughter who early in her childhood began having seizures. He said, "Dr. Freeman treated her, and now she's twenty-one and just graduated from college and living a normal life. I think the world of Dr. Freeman."

We were both overjoyed to hear such an inspiring testimony, but the man went on, "What other doctors do you see?"

I said, "Well, just Dr. Freeman. He's our doctor."

"You don't see any other doctors?"

I was surprised. "No, I mean, don't you just see Dr. Freeman?"

He looked astounded. "Why, no. Most of the time we see several other doctors." He looked at us as if marveling, then said, "How often do you see Dr. Freeman?"

"Um, about once every two weeks."

"Once every two weeks!"

I was feeling a little nonplussed, but I answered, "Well, how often do you see him?"

"Well, we make a long drive from Virginia each time, but we only saw Dr. Freeman about once a year, I guess. You know, he's head of the department."

I just swallowed and silently thanked God once again for the special provision He was making for us and Stasia.

Just two weeks later we were again in the Clinic, and a resident appeared and asked if we would answer some questions. He was obviously doing research in the Neurology Clinic, something very common at Johns Hopkins. We had plenty of time, so we agreed, and he began. About a minute into my first answer, Diana Pillas raced out of the hallway, burst into the room in a flurry, and said, "No-no-no-no-no!" shaking her hand at the resident and explaining, "No one sees the Kelleys! Just Dr. Freeman and me. No-no-no-no-no, you will not do this. No!"

The resident stared at her startled and obviously astounded. Johns Hopkins is a teaching hospital, and all patients normally had whole teams of doctors. Finally he said meekly, "I was just asking them a few questions. Can't I ask them just one question?"

Diana turned to me. She knew I was paranoid about Dr.

Freeman allowing any other doctor to see Stasia, so she said, "Is it okay?"

I said, "Sure."

She left, and the resident launched into a few more questions. After he finished with his research interview, he got up to walk out. Just before he reached the door, he stopped, turned, and with a rather puzzled look on his face said, "Do you mind if I ask you just one more question?"

I said, "Sure."

"How come you only see Dr. Freeman?"

I answered, now a little mystified myself, "We don't know. That's the way it's always been. Why do you find that so unusual?"

He said, "He's the chairman of the department. Most people only see him once a year."

I said, "Oh."

Again our gratitude only magnified. Later Diana would tell us, "The reason we invested so much time in you and Brian is because we both saw in you something worth saving, and we decided to do everything in our power to save it."

＊

Our last appointment before Christmas 1987 was a balmy, crisp day, and Stasia's cheeks were tinged slightly pink as she lay cuddled in her Christmas finery. I had ordered matching mother-daughter outfits from a specialty catalog. When we arrived, Diana, Georgia (the receptionist), and all the Clinic personnel who knew us scurried over to witness the latest spectacle of designer baby clothing. The banter around the Clinic was that Stasia never wore the same outfit twice—not precisely the truth, though close—and that Dr. Freeman and Diana had plans to hold a special sale of all of Stasia's gifts she'd only worn once to fund the new Pediatric Neurology wing. None of them could imagine how Brian could finance this prodigality, and I never told them that Brian's parents had willed over the family fortune in order to keep our little angel properly attired.

The meeting started as usual with a report about Stasia's condition. We were weaning Stasia off the prednisone and immediately informed Dr. Freeman that Stasia was now seizing upwards of forty or fifty times a day. From September to December we had worked at increasing the prednisone dosage, making numerous calls to Dr. Freeman about how high we should go. We charted out the seizures day by day with the lengths and times of each seizure. In early December we had reached the top threshold, and still the seizures continued. I wasn't overly concerned about it because I assumed Dr. Freeman would prescribe something else. In many ways I'd come to regard the doctor as the "family medical magician" who would fix whatever problems arose.

Dr. Freeman examined Stasia and asked more than the usual pointed questions about the seizures. He wanted to know everything about how they had affected her eating, her sleeping, her quiet times, everything. We gave him our charts, and this time he took copious notes, something that he did not usually do during our meetings. Diana sat quietly listening, making few comments.

After nearly an hour of discussion, Dr. Freeman stood as if he had remembered something he needed to do and left the room. He wasn't abrupt, and I assumed it meant nothing more than going out to retrieve an instrument or a chart or something related to our interview. He was gone about ten minutes. We learned much later he was so upset, he felt he had to leave the room.

When he came back into the room, we looked up at him hopefully. He said wearily, looking as if he'd aged in the ten minutes he'd been gone, "What I want you to do is to go home. I want you to have a great Christmas, and we'll set up an appointment in early January and talk then." He was seated, doodling with a pen. There was no eye contract.

I sat there stunned. I immediately sensed that something was terribly wrong. I was so alarmed and frightened, I could not go home on an ending like that. I said to him, "Don't do this ... Don't do this to us."

At that point Dr. Freeman got up. He knew I would pressure him until we got out of him what we wanted. But he said, "Go home, have a terrific Christmas, and we'll get together in January."

He moved to the door, and I called as he exited, "Don't do this, Dr. Freeman. Please don't do this!"

He didn't look back and didn't answer. I sat there with Diana and asked what was wrong. She said simply, "It doesn't look good at all."

Her words were so final, so negative, so sweeping. Where had they gotten such an idea? I wondered. I felt they must not understand. Stasia was eating better. She was gaining weight. She looked healthier and even more like a baby her age. I was certain this was a problem that could be overcome. Someday she'd be normal, or close to it. No one seemed to understand!

I had never doubted that Dr. Freeman could fix this thing. I still believed that if you gave not 100 percent, not 110 percent, but 200 percent or 300 percent of your very best, you could achieve anything. Give it all you've got and it is an absolute: the earth will move.

Often in the preceding months I'd fantasized that I would be one of those mothers you often read about with handicapped children who because of their extraordinary dedication, persistence, and superhuman effort enable their children to achieve things not even the experts dream are possible. I just knew I could be one of those mothers because if nothing else I was tenacious. Some might describe it as a stubborn streak a mile wide and three miles high. But every time Brian and I visited Dr. Freeman and engaged in one of these "doom talks," I would secretly smile to myself. I was convinced one day Dr. Freeman would look at me and say, "We never thought it was possible. What you've achieved with this child is a miracle."

I had even begun to believe this was God's purpose. It explained everything. Stasia was to be the means whereby God would stun the whole medical community. Stasia would show them once and for all there was something intangible in this medical business, something divine. Somehow God would leave His fingerprints all over it. It would be unmistakable, unquestionable. Through Brian, me, and Stasia, God would speak! Thus we would prove that the love of a child's family could work miracles. So long as the parents never ever gave up, the sky was the limit.

In those brief moments I had a glimmer of what was to come. But as always, I listened only to the inner thoughts I wanted to hear and ignored the others.

Holidays and
Something Special

I WAS OBSESSED with the questions raised by Dr. Freeman's words, and I was not looking forward to the holidays. But Brian encouraged me and tried hard to give us a semblance of normalcy. He put up the tree, decorated the house, and did most of the Christmas shopping. I was really in the doldrums. And then, on top of it all, my mother asked me, "Have you given any thought to having Stasia baptized?"

Immediately I knew she was right. The only reason we hadn't planned it earlier was because the pace of life was so hectic and we were still fighting for her life. Our appearances at church were a celebratory occasion for Dr. Adams.

December 19, 1987 turned out to be one of those days that starts in Hell and ends in Heaven. I had searched for a christening gown for months—I really wanted a handmade one, had even dreamed about such a thing since childhood, but no one stepped forward with an offer, and I couldn't find one locally, and had to finally settle for something I considered close to perfect. When Sunday arrived, I awoke as usual at 4 A.M. to begin getting Stasia ready. There was her bath, which usually took several hours, and her feeding, normally two to three more hours. As guests and family arrived about 10 A.M., I had nearly finished getting her dressed and ready for going out on that frigid wintry day—always a hazard and something that produced unparalleled tension in me with the fear of Stasia catching something.

No one, however, seemed to notice how much effort this was taking on my part. Brian was absorbed in his own morning libations, the family chatted away in the foyer, and my anger and resentment only grew. I felt as if it were me against them in the time crunch. No one offered a hand, or, more likely, I rebutted the offers and continued the chores with grim determination.

We had planned to make the eleven o'clock service. Brian's parents had arrived with his brother and sister-in-law, and their children stood about gawking, joking, and appearing for all intents and purposes to be preparing for a major festivity. My mother came to the door all decked out in a beaver fur and a matching pillbox hat. Everyone was ready to go, it would take us twenty minutes to get to the church, and we all stood in the foyer looking at Stasia. It was a real celebratory atmosphere.

Then suddenly Brian took a close look at me as if for the first time. I was still in my nightgown, wore no makeup, hadn't showered or brushed my disheveled hair. I felt like a half-crazed crone from the pit. My anger was reaching the boiling point as I realized there was no way I could get ready in time. Whatever anyone else might say, I am not one to go out in public without everything as close to perfect as I can get it. Brian just stared at me, a look of horror climbing up his features. "Alsie, you're not even dressed!"

Glaring at him, I answered coldly, "I know. Remember the baby—what it takes to get her ready?" I knew now there was no way I could personally get to the service in time. I moaned, "I've really had lots of help this morning."

My anger, though, touched something in Brian and instantly he was angry too—not at me, but at the situation. He knew Stasia's baptism was something I would rather die than miss. To have Brian's immediate and unquestioning support—I could see in his eyes how much he wanted "us" to share this "together"—quelled my anger, to my own surprise. Suddenly, whereas all that morning it had seemed to be me against them, now Brian and I were a team again, working toward the same goals and hopes. Nonetheless, I was positive I couldn't get ready in time. I said resignedly, really willing to give it up, "You all go ahead, and I'll do what I can, but if I miss it, I'll see you when you all get back."

Brian answered plaintively, "Please, Alsie, please try." He knew he had to leave now or no one would arrive in time. But his tone said he didn't want to go without me. The feelings of being neglected and of self-pity vanished. His sensitivity wiped it all away. The look in his eyes and his actions said this was a milestone the family absolutely had to share together.

He said again, "Your hair looks fine, you look great . . . Please try, Alsie. Please."

"Brian, this is a three-hour job here. I can't go like this."

"Alsie, please."

"Okay, I'll try." I was quite convinced we were facing Mission Impossible, but his insistent imploring had ignited something inside me.

Everyone left, and it was as if I suddenly sprouted wings. I actually took a shower, set my hair and dried it, and got everything else ready. I wonder if somehow God didn't compress time in some miraculous way, though not enough to keep me from breaking every speed limit as I got to the church at half-past 11. I learned later that when Brian had arrived with Stasia and the family to meet with the pastor before the service, Dr. Adams immediately decided to stall the baptism as long as possible in hopes that I'd get there in time. People later remarked that his announcements and commentary seemed to stretch on for hours as he worked to stave off the possibility of my not arriving in time. I found the family waiting in the church office. Just as Dr. Adams had begun to run out of announcements about events well into the next year, we all marched in and sat down in a back pew.

Stasia's baptismal gown was made of white satin, inlaid with lace. It had a full-length coat and bonnet that matched the dress. I had her wrapped in a fluffy white blanket. Dr. Adams called us up front. He always introduced a baptism with some personal words about the baby and family, so he began with a few comments about the meaning of Stasia's name—Anastasia, which in Greek means "resurrection"—and then moved on to an inspiring speech about the church and its need to unify behind and prayerfully support all families with little children. "This is what inclusion in the covenant family is about," he said, "and by your witnessing and participating in this event, you are offering your own love and friendship to this little girl and her parents."

He spoke of Stasia's condition and how great our own struggle was just to "get through the day" and to "keep the household on some level of normalcy." He commented that we had been given a difficult task such as only God could give, but one in which, by His grace, we would not fail. His words were powerful and touching. He soon had me, Brian, and, it seemed, most of those present in tears.

Dr. Adams finished, his own voice shaking with emotion, by saying, "This child was given to the only two people who could take care of her." I knew he meant not that we were the best parents in the world, but that Stasia had been hand-picked for us, and we for her, one more expression of his own convictions about God's sovereignty and wisdom. It was another of those divinely appointed encouragements that would remain with me ever after.

Finally he asked the whole congregation to stand—as we always do in our church for baptisms—and "pledge our support to this special family." Amazingly, I felt a unity, a kinship, and a love flowing over me from the congregation like a great river of divine refreshment so that we all seemed momentarily lifted up to Heaven.

Then it was over, and we returned to the back pew, but I could not stop weeping, so Brian and I went back to the church office to sit and talk quietly about all that had just happened. Afterwards we all drove home and opened our house to family and friends from the church. It was the first time we'd had a large group in the house since Stasia had been born, and the warmth of their love and fellowship seemed to carry us along in a joyous ride into real happiness.

Everything looked so beautiful and smelled so fragrant. The house looked festive. The sun shone through the windows in fine slats of yellow and gold. We were surrounded by friends and loved ones. For the first time it really did feel like Christmas.

*

The January appointment with Dr. Freeman finally arrived. We had tried hard to enjoy Stasia's first Christmas, and certainly her baptism had been a real highlight. However, behind every surfacing hope and every glimmer of joy lurked the feeling that Dr. Freeman was going to drop another bomb like he had last September. Nonetheless, we really couldn't conceive of anything worse than we had already heard.

Diana led us into the treatment room at the Clinic and had us both sit down. I picked Stasia up out of the carriage and held her. Brian and I were both extremely anxious, wondering what was coming. Diana began the meeting with small talk about the holiday, and we told her about the baptism. She asked if we had pictures—Brian used to joke that anyone looking for a new stock should try Kodak; we were tearing through two rolls a week at that point—and I quickly found the latest batch in my pocketbook. After looking over the photos and offering some eloquent compliments about the dress and everything else, she joked, "Would you two adopt me? I really need a wardrobe like this!" Our spirits revived just in the retelling, but finally Brian said in a more solemn vein, "We've been very worried about what Dr. Freeman is going to tell us now."

Diana looked pained. She said, "Dr. Freeman will explain every-thing, but I should prepare you—it's not good."

Dr. Freeman arrived, and again we talked about the seizures. He told us, "We cannot control the seizures."

I asked, "Isn't there some other medication we can try?"

"If Stasia were a healthy adult like you or me and had a job and had to drive a car, the risk of her suffering a seizure while driving or working would justify putting her on a stronger medication and risking the accompanying side effects. The stronger the medica-tion, the more serious the side effects. I'm talking here about the quality of life. For example, if you were to have a seizure while driv-ing a car you could and probably would be killed. If you were out shopping and experienced a seizure, you might very well injure yourself seriously when you fell. Thus any side effects or at least all but the most severe would be bearable given the quality of life you were able to enjoy while using the medication. It's always a trade-off. Benefits against side effects. For Stasia—" Here he paused, choosing his words very carefully. "—the benefits would be mini-mal if not nonexistent when weighed against the side effects."

"What do you mean 'minimal'?" I asked.

"Stasia cannot walk, talk, or even sit up, much less crawl, run or care for herself in any way."

"But she *will* be able to do those things one day," I insisted. "We'll teach her, no matter how long it takes or how hard we have to work. Don't write her off yet," I cried.

"I'm not writing her off, and believe me when I tell you it's not a question of time or effort. How I wish with all my heart that it were. No one knows better than Diana and I what you two would sacrifice for this lucky little girl," he said.

Again I tried. "I tell you, she *will* be able to do these things! She *will!* I just need time."

Dr. Freeman leaned forward, gazing steadily into my eyes. "No, Alsie, she will never be able to walk, talk, sit up or care for herself in any way. In fact, she will probably never progress beyond the level of a two-month-old."

Tears began spilling over my cheeks into my lap. I could no longer control them. "So now what?" I whispered.

Dr. Freeman answered quietly, "What we need to be concerned about now is making Stasia as comfortable as possible. I'm going to try her on Phenobarbitol and see how she responds."

"And then what can we expect?"

"If the seizures continue to increase, she will only deteriorate."

Somehow I managed, "Then this is as good as it gets, the level of a two-month-old?"

He nodded, as if keeping himself under tight, almost rigid control. "I'm afraid that's right."

I murmured, "What about life expectancy?"

"It's really difficult to say. It could be a year. It could be two. It could be three. Little Herbie Poole lived to . . ." He glanced over at Diana who mouthed a number. "Herbie lived to be nine. So I honestly can't give you a number."

As the final realization struck me, I choked out the terrible words, "How does it usually happen?"

Dr. Freeman looked infinitely weary. He was still sitting in front of me, this man on whom I'd put the weight of the world. He wasn't at all diminished in my eyes, but I realized even he could do nothing more. He said quietly, "Usually pneumonia or cardiac arrest."

As silence filled the room, we sat looking from Dr. Freeman to Diana, thinking one of them would offer some hidden hope they had reserved for just this moment. But nothing was offered. Brian had been holding my hand—as he always did—and he gave it a squeeze. Instantly the tears filled my eyes again, and I looked down at Stasia in my arms.

Diana said, "Alsie?"

My eyes met hers, and she said fervently, "Alsie, you're not alone in this. We're all going to see this through together."

I knew she was absolutely sincere. I thought back to Christmas and the baptism and all those hours wondering what Dr. Freeman could possibly reveal that might be worse. Now here it was, something I had not allowed myself to anticipate. We talked some more, both of them repeating their assurances, and when we felt able to leave the room, Dr. Freeman said, "Why don't we make an appointment for a month or six weeks . . ."

I instantly replied, "No, two weeks . . . It has to be two weeks. Every time we go longer, something bad happens."

He looked at me with an understanding smile on his face, then turned to Diana. "Am I traveling or anything in the next two weeks? Do we have an opening?"

I said, "Dr. Freeman, you can't go anywhere!"

He cocked his head, probably both incredulous and amused, then said, "All right . . . Diana, make sure there's an opening in two weeks."

Somehow Brian and I both sensed that after today our lives would never be the same again. Looking back, I believe God sent these two people to us to bring some order out of the chaos that had become our daily lives. Our world and our relationship as we knew it was shattering. It had ceased to exist. Whatever was to follow, whether to carve out a whole new existence from the ashes of the old, or simply to give up and slowly disintegrate as our hopes and dreams and our miracle child seemed destined to do, was largely in Dr. Freeman's and Diana's hands. These two people who poured so much of themselves and their time and their effort into Brian and me, and their unshakable faith in us and our ability to see this through is what kept us going through the darkest and most difficult times. We simply could not disappoint them.

*

We took Stasia home, feeling a new and crueler sentence of death hanging over us. In my fantasies of the baby's miraculous recovery at least I had been able to find some solace. But now reality had struck, and there was no evading it. All the early depression and bitterness exploded over the next few days. I changed inside, growing angrier and more and more depressed. One day Brian came back from work and asked me how I was doing.

I retorted, "Fine . . . just fine."

"What does that mean?"

"How am I supposed to feel? When I look into the future, I see a black hole. When this child dies, I die."

I felt more responsible for Stasia's handicaps than ever. Though every doctor we'd talked to assured me repeatedly that the antibiotic I'd taken before I knew I was pregnant couldn't possibly have caused Stasia's condition, I argued, "She came from my body; I must somehow be responsible."

At the same time a reverse belief infused me: God, if He wanted to, could heal Stasia. He could take her home through death, or she could get well. I began playing with two words in my mind: "God could heal her, but would He?" "Could" and "would" jumped back and forth inside me like Ping-Pong balls.

What I couldn't understand was this in-between state of no improvement, steady deterioration, and a slow but certain death. Why did God seem to sit and do nothing?

Those two questions ground away in my mind: If God could do something, then why didn't He? And if He wasn't planning to do something incredible, why had He even allowed it to happen in the first place?

Neither I nor Brian had any answer, and I hadn't found it in my faith, even though I looked for it constantly. I kept coming across all the truths about God's mercy and how He loved little children and had even said, "Except you become as a little child, you will not enter the kingdom of heaven." That verse resounded in my mind like thunder. If that was true, then little children had a special place in His Kingdom. But none of it fit in with what I was seeing in my home. I kept saying, "A loving God wouldn't do this."

Stasia's Gift

And thus, since it had so obviously happened, the conclusion was: Is there a God at all?

Something had to break. I only hoped it wasn't us.

82

Little Things

STASIA'S SEIZURES CONTINUED to escalate, fifty, then sixty, up to eighty a day. She wasn't sleeping except in little cat-naps. She exhibited a tense crankiness that had us all on edge. She was off the prednisone completely, and Dr. Freeman prescribed Phenobarbital to help "manage" the seizures, which at this point was the best he could do.

One thing we had resisted all along was Dr. Freeman's suggestion to use chloral hydrate to sedate Stasia at night so she could sleep until morning. Neither Brian nor I could abide the idea of "knocking out" our daughter so we could sleep. I referred to such an idea as "barbaric." In effect, I wouldn't even listen to any talk about what *we* needed; Stasia was my complete focus. But finally Dr. Freeman impressed upon us that this was not just for us, but for Stasia. She needed rest. Until then it had seemed to me that Dr. Freeman was always more concerned about us than about her. It was nearly an adversarial position. But now I realized that Dr. Freeman saw us all as one unit, and he was treating us and Stasia together as if we were one single persona. He reiterated, "The better you take care of you, the better you'll take care of her." I was skeptical, so he tried again, this time hitting closer to home. "If anything happens to you, who'll take care of her?" That worked.

One night we reached our limit; so we decided to try the sedative. The next morning we awoke refreshed, and so did Stasia. The crankiness ceased, and she appeared rested, serene, and more alert than she had in months. It was such a dramatic turnaround, I was truly amazed. From that time we used the chloral hydrate regularly, and Stasia began to get the rest she so desperately needed.

During this time we developed a morning routine that kept both Brian and me occupied for the first few hours of the day. I sensed we were working together as a team again, and in fact it would become the one aspect of our life that held us together through the storms ahead. It also gave me the opportunity to pour out all the love I felt for my daughter, thinking these few simple tasks would somehow convey to her the depth of my love. The pace of my day kept me in constant motion as I determined to still be the best mother Stasia could ever have.

First, her eyes had to be cleaned and washed. Her tear ducts did not work properly, and a hardened mucus formed if her eyes weren't cleaned every morning, afternoon, and night.

When her teeth began coming in, they had to be brushed with special care and gentleness because Stasia was so sensitive to touch. Additionally, since she had no idea what we were trying to accomplish with this ritual, but she liked the taste of toothpaste, she assumed it was breakfast and kept trying to bite the toothbrush. It usually wasn't too difficult to insert the toothbrush in her mouth, but then the tricky part was would she let you brush her teeth and if and when you were finished could you remove it!

Next, her nose and throat had to be suctioned out. Stasia suffered from repeated sinus problems, also as a result of her birth defects. A sinus infection was treated with Intensive Care Unit concern.

Each morning I administered a battery of vitamins before she ate. It was all the more crucial because we discovered that her body failed to assimilate and use normal formula quantities of vitamins E, A, C, D, and B-12, to name a few.

Of course, there was always the changing of diapers, but the need to inspect stools for internal bleeding made the job that much more meticulous.

I entered into all these activities with my normal "all-out" attitude, her needs taking precedence over all others. In particular, I longed to see a response from Stasia to our care. Dr. Freeman had warned us that Stasia was incapable of any thought processes whatsoever. The litany—"she will never walk, talk, or do anything for herself, ever"—was played over and over in my mind. Even a smile would have been encouraging. But according to tests, the doctors weren't sure if Stasia could see much less process any stimuli as a normal nine-month-old would.

Still, I was convinced something was going on inside her. At times she would slowly raise her arms in reaction to a touch or a kiss. She pursed her lips at times, and in response to a sound or a door closing, her eyes would widen, and sometimes she would even jump at a yell, as if she were startled. I looked and waited continually for a sign of something, anything, that would show she knew me or Brian, or at least was happy and comfortable. But except for the time when she had cried incessantly because of the double hernia, she never made any noises of discomfort or desire. She didn't even let us know when she was hungry; I had to guess.

All this discouraged me deeply and made me feel all the more guilty as the one who had possibly caused all this through some malfunction of my body when she was in my womb.

Each day, of course, there was the need to sterilize everything that touched Stasia's lips. Nipples, pacifiers, and syringes were all boiled on the stove before any of the other morning chores could be done. This wasn't just "first mother" paranoia. Stasia was vulnerable to a plethora of illnesses that any normal baby could ward off with hardly a sign of discomfort or distress. Stasia's immune system was already known to be weak; on a scale of 10, it was ranked about 2. We lived in constant fear that a sinus infection would escalate into the dreaded pneumonia.

Finally, there was the feeding. Her sucking abilities were

extremely weak. The feeble efforts she could make quickly tired her. She was subject to choking on even the most minute swallows of formula that entered her throat. Thus, it took from two to three hours to get two ounces of formula into her. At only seven pounds, she desperately needed to gain weight in order to withstand the surgical procedures that might later solve some of the major problems.

Brian would place Stasia in my arms amid a bevy of pillows. Stasia was like the princess who could not abide a pea under twenty mattresses. We used the pillows to get her comfortable; otherwise, she would fuss and not eat.

Once settled, the feeding would begin. Brian would bring me my cup of tea and a muffin, cooked to perfection (Brian made me say that), and finally the bottle and baby food. I would feed Stasia, and for once I could see a genuine response. She would not swallow food she didn't like—peas, green beans, lima beans, anything green, and didn't like meat unless it had syrup on it. For me, it was exhilarating to watch her eyes get big and happy as she downed something she enjoyed. At that time I felt like a normal mother. It was the only period in her entire life where she gave a definite response to something we did. I loved the whole process.

When we were happily situated, Brian left for work. The two- to three-hour process of feeding went on three times a day. It became a sacrosanct time, a secure period of Stasia's life that I could count on for its peace and length. It was the one time I knew I'd be alone with the baby and my thoughts for hours on end without interruption. It was also a time of peace and tranquillity, despite the questions that bounced through my mind about our predicament.

Because of the birth defects, Stasia also suffered from numerous physical deformities. We were assured by various doctors that she was not in pain, but we still went to great lengths to accommodate her. She had no body or head control and would literally be a two-month-old baby all her life. We used an "egg-crate" mattress cut up into different sizes for a crib and also changing tables and even my lap. This helped a lot.

The worst problem was scoliosis of the spine, which caused her spinal column to grow into an S-curve. She had three malformed vertebrae that the doctors said could be removed; by fusing the spine and using other procedures they might later be able to correct the condition. But it was major surgery and very risky.

Stasia was also afflicted with severe muscle contractures on her right side. This meant that those muscles were extremely tight, causing her to hunch her shoulders rigidly under her chin, hold her right arm flexed over her stomach, and clench both hands into fists. Stasia's hips were also dislocated, and our doctors told us that could be fixed by an operation as well.

Finally, Stasia's right foot was crooked, a twisting of the instep that looked painful even though the doctors said it wasn't.

Because of all these problems, we saw a battery of doctors besides Dr. Freeman. Dr. Scott Strahlmann at Columbia Medical Plan, Stasia's pediatrician, specialized in handicapped children. We visited the renowned Kennedy Institute next to Johns Hopkins for physical therapy weekly. Dr. Paul Sponseller, an orthopedic surgeon, examined Stasia's back and hips. We also saw specialists in gastro-enterology at Johns Hopkins and in ophthalmology at Columbia Medical, as well as private practitioners in podiatry and nutrition. We were in doctor's offices an average of two to three times a week. We soon began affectionately referring to this conglomerate of doctors as "the Kelley Team."

The question always before us and the doctors was whether all these problems were physically or neurologically caused. If it was solely a physical problem, surgery could correct all of it. But if we discovered it was neurological, no amount of surgery could permanently change anything. Our prayer was that it was indeed all physiological.

As you might imagine, all this produced a high level of concentration simply in picking her up. It normally took two people to handle her and move her because of all the adjustments one made in watching out for her head, back, hips, and legs. To alleviate her discomfort, though, we soon learned to use a mass of pillows to situate her wherever she lay. This marvelous array of pillows, blankets, and stuffed animals tucked under and around her was carefully arranged and adjusted by both me and Brian so that Stasia found a point of comfort and settled down. Of course, whatever adjustments Brian made, I always quickly readjusted until they were unequivocally perfect! The indicator was the baby's quiet calm, her eyes unfocused but staring about, waiting for the "big moment." On top of this pile, Stasia resembled some Indian princess, and we soon gave her the nickname "the little Pasha." It was another of those "little moments" for which we felt gratitude. Not everyone had a "little Pasha" in their home.

It was always remarkable to me, though, that Stasia, despite these numerous problems and handicaps, always seemed so at peace. Even with only 10 percent of her brain, I believed sometime there would occur some mother-daughter communication. I was already learning to read some of her minute responses as indications of distress, fear, or pleasure, so I was certain something was going on inside her.

As I struggled with my anger at God and some of the bitterness I felt during that first year, both Brian and I began to discover a kind of joy in "small things." For instance, each morning as light dawned, I would awaken and lie in bed savoring the last few moments of rest before the marathon of the day. Often I would zero in and listen to Stasia's breathing through the baby monitor. I was awaiting what I'd come to think of as "the signal."

Each morning after a brief period of quiet, Stasia uttered "the signal." It was a one syllable "hah!"—high-pitched, even loud in the quiet of the house. It was as though she was saying, "I'm here! I'm awake! Come get me!"

I came to cherish those moments each morning and would literally lie there in a state of suspense, wondering when the signal would sound. An electric bolt of joy and thrill would resound in my own heart as I heard it, and Brian would bound out of bed as if sprung from a trap. He would go in, pick up Stasia, and bring her in to lie between us. Then he would return to the bliss of another hour of sleep while I lay there terrified I'd drift off and roll over onto her.

Stasia's favorite time of day was her bath in the kitchen. The water had to be heated to just the right temperature because she was very sensitive to abrupt changes in heat and cold. An aloe vera creme was set to warm in a glass of hot water. Next the towels we'd use to dry her off were heated by opening the oven door and draping them over the space between the door and the stove. After that, her day's outfit was laid over the towels so they also would be warm when Stasia was ready to be dressed. The whole house was regulated to insure proper temperature—turning off the air conditioning in the summer and turning up the heat in the winter. Finally, a bubble bath was added to the bathwater to give Stasia what I considered a necessary requisite for any sophisticated woman's libations.

As I set her in the bath on a rather complicated arrangement of a body-size sponge and washcloths designed to keep her comfortable, she looked totally at peace. It was an almost euphoric look on her face that I'm convinced would have made a great television commercial for bath salts. In a word, she loved it.

Afterwards, Stasia was extremely relaxed, and we rubbed her down with the warmed creme and performed her physical therapy. This involved manipulating all her limbs to loosen up the muscles. We found that if we did it while singing whatever came to mind, mostly nonsensical made-up, on-the-spot songs, she cooperated much more readily. We learned that as we cooed, "One-two-three-whee" and "Soooooo big," she got to the point where she would actually raise her arms on her own (even though Dr. Freeman denied it was anything more than an involuntary motor response and dubbed it "another mother's fantasy"). For me, though, my mother's instincts were greatly heartened by her obvious pleasure. It was a refreshment, an oasis in an otherwise hectic, stress-filled day.

These were the three primary "little things" we came to look forward to and appreciate with deep gratitude. It gave me tremendous satisfaction to know that I could actually do something that would bring Stasia pleasure. While parents of normal babies could expect far more noise, smiles, playful touches, coos, giggles, and laughs, Brian and I realized the morning "signal," her feedings, and the bath might be the limits of communication Stasia could reach for. I began to think of them as tiny examples of God's grace and love toward us. He was teaching us appreciation of His creation, and especially of children, on an entirely new plane of existence. For all of us our world at times seems to concentrate only on the "big noises" of life—the Nobels, Pulitzers, "breakthroughs," Super Bowls, and so many other of those triumphs we label "significant." But here I was looking forward to a single sound at the start of a long day, a few teaspoons of baby food, and the bath of a child who was not able to give the minutest verbal response. I was learning to observe her in ways that were virtually microscopic, and in the process I detected a multitude of tiny expressions of both discomfort and pleasure that formed the basis of our communication.

It was for me a powerful insight and a moment of transformation. Something was happening in me, even though at the time I might not have realized it. Though it did not dissipate all my inner pain, it was a real source of joy in the daily routine. It was just one more sign that despite the problems, despite the destiny that doctors had said awaited our little one, despite the pain and fear and anguish and guilt, Stasia was ours, our child, our little girl, and nothing could induce me or Brian to exchange her for someone of greater abilities and intelligence.

A First

NONETHELESS, DESPITE THE SPARKS of joy that flickered occasionally throughout the day, I entered a suicidal period, and Brian withdrew into his own thoughts through silence. Prior to this, we had shared everything in life. Some of our friends told me we were "perpetual honeymooners," often sharing our dreams and thoughts in the evening as we sat together in the family room or ate dinner or breakfast. I loved being married, and Brian was truly a source of incredible exhilaration in my life.

While still childless, we had discovered a special kinship in our mutual love of family, church, community, reading, and friends. We each had our individual interests, but we did almost everything together, and I knew we deeply loved one another, readily sharing our deepest thoughts without fear of rejection or indifference. Frequently, even after being married for seven years, when we went somewhere on a vacation people would ask us if we were on our honeymoon. We always held hands, laughed, and took great pleasure in one another.

Unfortunately, with the insecurity of the new world whose center was Stasia, both of us forged ahead separately, retreating into isolated places and thoughts, each of us trying to make sense of all that had happened in our own way. Communication between us suffered a slow death. We were worn-out, overwhelmed with sadness and self-pity. Brian in particular felt his role as a father was completely stymied. He could do nothing to "fix" this, and I sensed he was either unwilling or unable to deal with his feelings of impotence.

Inside both of us reigned an acute feeling of dreams that had been shattered and disintegrated. We had planned it all out so carefully during those years of waiting to conceive—through discussions about schools, lessons, and all the paraphernalia of childhood . . . DisneyWorld . . . Baltimore Orioles games . . . Sandi Patti concerts . . . Nursery school . . . Kindergarten . . . Monopoly games . . . Talks on the phone . . . College . . . All the great questions of growing up.

Now it was all gone. It would never happen, at least not with Stasia. Those hopes and dreams had been swept away by Dr. Freeman's grim words: "She'll never walk. She'll never talk. She'll never even smile. She only has 10 percent of her brain, and she'll be on the level of a two-month-old for the rest of her life."

I embarked upon a period where I prayed over Stasia in the crib each night, asking God to "see her safely through the night," or if He chose to take her home, to "take her gently and mercifully." This was not a copout or a desire to escape my own responsibilities. Rather, I honestly felt He could take much better care of her than I could. The idea of providing for Stasia on the level required daunted me to the point of depression and despair.

God didn't take Stasia, though, and Dr. Freeman and our other doctors assured us her heart and lungs were sound and strong.

That prayer unanswered, I then began to ask that He would take me. I started driving without a seat belt and drove somewhat recklessly when Stasia wasn't with me. I would plunge into traffic situations where caution was the wiser side of courage. Often I contemplated various ways of ending my life—something painless, it had to be painless—like overdosing on sleeping pills or the baby's phenobarbital.

For me, this was a strange, even bizarre mode of thought. I have always been a fighter who finds a way to win—sometimes against formidable odds. I fervently believed in the principle of "give it all you've got and you'll succeed."

But Stasia's disability was a problem I saw no way around or through. Fortunately, Brian recognized these dark moods for what they were and often tried to humor me out of them, keying in on my perfectionism. I was especially obsessive about how Stasia looked and did all in my power to dress her beautifully. It was, in a sense, the one area which I could completely control as her mother, and it made me feel good to receive others' compliments and to walk into the Clinic with everyone clamoring, "Oh, bring her over . . . Let's see what she's wearing today!"

Knowing how important this was to me, Brian would comment when he heard me talking about ending it all, "If you go away, I'll never iron her clothes. She'll go out with her dress buttoned backwards." Or he'd shout, "I'd probably take her out with a dirty face." Or, "I would never buy her new clothes. She'd just have the same old ones. All the time. Forever!"

At times I even managed a laugh. I was so compulsive about those things that his words had just enough connection with reality to bring me back to earth.

Yet, despite these little asides and moments of levity, things were falling apart between Brian and me. He would "vege" out in front of the television the moment he got home, leaving me to care for the baby—primarily because he couldn't do anything to suit me where Stasia was concerned. He didn't say so, but he felt useless, like he was no longer a part of my or Stasia's life. At the time I didn't realize a lot of his passivity was because of my own unwillingness to let him be a part of anything.

At the same time, while I began wrestling with the deeper theological issues, Brian was just plain angry and bitter. I'd ask him why he didn't pray or go to church anymore. He would reply, "God and I don't have a lot to talk about these days." If I probed him about it, he would answer, "My job stinks. My marriage stinks. My daughter is dying. What do God and I have to talk about?" Once he took the Sunday paper with him to church and threatened to read it in the back pew while the service was going on—just to aggravate me! My perception was that all he did was eat, sleep, watch television, and perform the few chores I asked him to do.

In reality, Brian was doing a lot for Stasia, mostly when I wasn't there to observe it. When I asked him to do anything, he would do precisely what I asked—because I often criticized every move he made with the baby. However, when he was alone with Stasia, he would spend hours with her during her bath, singing made-up songs, feeding her, changing her, and actually enjoying it all in ways that I had missed entirely. In three years he never missed a single doctor's appointment we knew was important. On occasion he awakened before I did, got Stasia up, and began the whole morning routine before I was even conscious. Yet, because of my own concentration on Stasia and my responsibility to her, I saw little of this at the time for what it was.

We would realize later that this was something that inevitably happens under such circumstances. Our perceptions became skewed, and we began to attack one another on the basis of those faulty perceptions. It was something both Dr. Freeman and Diana quickly recognized and did all they could to stop.

That was the lowest point of our marriage. Frequently I said to Brian, "Our life is over. Our marriage is over. When this child dies, I die. There will be no reason for me to live after that." I simply wanted to wake up in Heaven and forget the pain and horror of this world.

But two things kept me going. One was plain ego. I really did not think any other person could or would give Stasia the time, care, and love that I could as her biological mother.

The other was the encouragement of people like Reverend Adams and Annette and Suzy and others from the church, but especially Diana and Dr. Freeman. I could not escape the fact that they all seemed to care that we succeeded as parents and as a couple. I honestly felt that if I gave up, took the sleeping pills, or packed up and just disappeared, I would be letting them down. For so many years I'd felt I had to be perfect in order to be loved. When all these people continued to love me despite my obvious imperfections, I knew I could not disappoint them. They kept telling me what a terrific mother I was; it was rare that anyone gave me that level of sincere affirmation. I simply could not let them down.

Then things did get better. Stasia passed her first year in May 1988. On July 4 of that summer, Stasia gave me something I'd waited for and prayed for nearly every day for the past year—her first smile. She always had poor control of her facial muscles. Her eyes rarely focused. Even Dr. Freeman said she'd probably never smile. Stasia had been gaining weight bit by bit and growing, but she still hadn't done anything normal babies do: no "Mamas" or "Papas" fell from her lips; no first steps; no playful grins or smiles at a tickle or caress.

Then on the morning of July 4th, as I waited in the recliner for Brian to bring her breakfast, Stasia shone like a beacon in a storm. I peered down at the little bundle. Gazing up at me were those two beautiful blue eyes and an ear-splitting grin that neither I nor Brian had ever witnessed before.

Barely daring to breathe and perhaps disturb the quiet glow, I called to Brian, "Get over here immediately!"

Stasia didn't let up. Dr. Freeman had been so sure she would never have the control to project a real smile, even a flickering one. And here was this lightning-bolt grin almost set in stone. It was beautiful, touching, one of those moments you store in your mind's eye for the rest of your life.

With Stasia still grinning up at me as if I were the best mommy in the whole wide world, we both began to talk at once.

"What an angel!"

"They said it wasn't possible."

"The very first one!"

Meanwhile, Brian ran to get the camera. A few moments later we had the moment memorialized on film, a whole roll's worth. This was "proof" of I don't know what, but I decided to corral Dr. Freeman next visit and see what he said. He only grinned and joked that it was probably gas, adding, "What great lengths these mothers go to to prove their doctors wrong," but he seemed genuinely pleased that I was so obviously excited and feeling better. Those two "true blues" offering that "special look" Brian said she reserved only for me, and that smile effervescing all the way down to her toes, made my day—maybe my year! It remains one of our most profound and fond memories.

Still, that wasn't the end. The same day, we all journeyed to Mom's house and spent the day cooking and celebrating in a July 4th cookout. And Stasia kept smiling. It was as though she'd chosen this moment to give us all a gift we'd hoped for, and then she'd multiplied it to maximum impact. Not just a smile, but a regular hootin' hollarin' hullabaloo of a smile that put everyone six feet above the pavement.

This was another hint at the possibility of hope. Regardless of what the doctors said, I took this as Stasia's recognition of me personally as her mother. I lived on it for months. It was another step in my own emotional and spiritual rehabilitation.

Around this time I also discovered that Stasia responded to music; in fact, she loved it. One of her favorites was "Brahms' Lullaby," which I frequently sang as I sat with Stasia long hours day in and day out in the family room. When friends would ask what kind of present Stasia might like, it was always a new music box. She had several that played the "Lullaby," a turtle that played "It's a Small World," and a white bear in a red hat with "Stasia" embroidered on it and a red heart that lights up. We called him "Christmas Bear," and he performed a medley of Christmas carols, a least a dozen.

I might set Stasia down on the changing table or on the couch billowed up on a cloud of pillows, and if any music box was turned on close to her ear, Stasia would shift her eyes in the direction of the sound. There was a stillness about her as she listened. Brian always sang to her during her bath, singing to sixties and seventies rock tunes, but replacing the lyrics with endless repetitions of "Scooby-doo." Whenever Stasia was going through some major stress or illness, especially during visits to the hospital, I would hum the "Lullaby" over and over softly into her ear, and it would inevitably calm her, frequently putting her to sleep.

I began to think of these moments as "little gifts" and "surprises" God was showering upon us as expressions of His love. There was the morning "Hah." And the bath. And now the smile and her response to music. I'd gaze into her eyes and sense that something great was going on inside her, as if she were truly a little angel locked in a broken body but still struggling to proclaim the glory of God.

We also noticed that Stasia began giving individualized responses to different people. When Brian arrived home from work and inevitably found me and Stasia ensconced in one another's arms in the rocking chair in the corner of the family room, he would bend down and whisper in Stasia's ear, "Daddy's home." Stasia would shift her eyes all the way around toward him. Her arms and legs became very animated, as if she were trying to run to him. She even pursed her lips as though trying to say something. Because of the muscle contractures on her right side, she couldn't twist her head around to look at him. But the motion in her eyes and limbs told it all.

Often as I hummed the "Lullaby" after a long day, Stasia would blink herself to sleep and finally settle down into a soft slumber.

Brian told me Stasia also reserved a look for me that she never gave anyone else. Repeatedly I would ask Brian, "Do you think she loves me?" Brian always replied, "If you could see the look she gives you like I do, you'd know. It's a look of such peace and happiness. I know she loves you."

My mother was the only one who could put Stasia to sleep when she was agitated. One of those grandmothers with just the right "soft spots," Mom seemed able to make Stasia feel safe and secure.

Stasia loved human contact, but rarely responded to other stimuli. Give an infant a toy, a pen, a set of keys, and they'll frolic with it for hours, bang it on the edge of the crib, and scream joy all over the continent about it. But Stasia would never hold onto anything that wasn't human. Give her your finger and she'd clasp it firmly and tightly. But place a pencil in her hand and there was no response.

We discovered how acute Stasia's sense of smell was when the head of the Baltimore County Special Education Department, Ruth Anderson, visited us to teach and test Stasia with "infant stimulation" toys. We had discovered that all handicapped children in Maryland are entitled to special education from birth. One of the tests involved dipping cotton balls in food flavorings. Stasia wasn't much on coconut, mint, or almond, but orange made her smack her lips noisily.

The problems were still very real. I was physically worn-out. Stasia still was not sleeping well through the night. When she did sleep, Brian would let me grab a minute's sleep and would say, "Sleep fast." It became a pet saying around the house, but something also that held us together, one of those personal rituals we could laugh about in our happier moments, but which also sealed what was left of intimacy in our marriage.

Something Almost
Too Simple

DESPITE THE FACT that things were improving, I still felt overwhelmed by Stasia's extraordinary needs and my inability to meet them. My own insecurities began to come out in the idea that if Dr. Freeman decided I really wasn't capable of taking care of Stasia properly, he would institutionalize her and take her away from us forever. I thought that if I always looked competent, in control, rested, and flawlessly groomed, no one would notice what I believed were my very obvious inadequacies as the mother of a handicapped child. Thus, I learned to look perfect for Dr. Freeman.

Normally I'm sure I looked to Brian like "the wrath of God" around the house, rarely applying makeup or doing my hair. There just wasn't time, even though this was against my every instinct prior to becoming a mother. The days we had appointments with Dr. Freeman at the Clinic, though, I spent most of the morning getting ready. I was often so nervous on the way to the Clinic that Brian could not understand what the problem was. Finally, after several discussions, he discovered my deep-rooted fear of losing Stasia through a command from the authorities to give her to those who could really and truly meet her needs.

I always dressed my best for Dr. Freeman, knowing he would demand to know how things were really going. Moreover, I determined to present to him the most effervescent and happy face I could muster to show that everything was well, even to the point of concealing the truth.

His first question at our biweekly conferences was usually, "How's it going, Alsie?" Inevitably I'd smile and reply with what I thought was radiant enthusiasm: "Great, just great!"

Dr. Freeman would frown, gaze at me insightfully as if searching for the truth, then say again, "How's it going, Alsie?"

"Everything is great, Dr. Freeman. Really."

After several go-rounds of this, with a look of frustration etched on his face he would finally turn to Brian. "How's it really going, Brian?"

Brian wouldn't speak. He'd simply hold up his hand and make a gesture indicating, "So-so," though that was painting a happy face on it. In reality we were barely talking, I was exhausted, and Brian was frustrated at my constantly criticizing him about every effort he made.

Realizing how bad things were, Dr. Freeman would tell Brian, "Will you please see that this woman gets out? Take her to a restaurant or a movie—anything. Get her out of that house. Get a baby-sitter. I'll even pay for it." He'd dramatically reach for his billfold. But Brian would say, "We're working on it, doctor."

Dr. Freeman would look back at me and shake his head with sincere concern. "You've got to hold your marriage together, Alsie. You have to give your husband and yourself time, too."

Immediately the protests would start. "Dr. Freeman, there is no time."

"Rubbish! You can't take care of the baby if you don't take care of yourself. I don't want to see you again until I'm convinced you're spending some time away from that house, and I'm going to ask Brian if you're faking it. Got it?"

I would finally sigh, "Okay," wondering how few minutes out of the house were necessary to satisfy this outlandish requirement.

This scene was repeated many many times over that first year as Dr. Freeman kept trying to get a true fix on what was going on in our home and inside each of us. It was in one of these sessions that Dr. Freeman suddenly lanced the deep fear that had been dragging away inside me. He stopped the initial routine about how I was doing, turned to Brian, and said, "Why does she persist in saying she's great when things so obviously aren't?"

Brian paused, then said very quietly, "She's afraid you're going to take the baby away and put her in an institution."

I was so stunned that Brian would blurt this out that I was speechless. Tears slid out of my eyes as I looked at Stasia in my arms, sure Dr. Freeman was about to wrest her from me and send her off to that place where she'd get the kind of care she really needed. But Dr. Freeman only sat back in his seat and exclaimed, "What?" He looked hard at me despite my tears and said, "Where would you get an idea like that?"

I didn't want to answer. But Dr. Freeman waited patiently until I spoke. I said, "I'm not very good at this, Dr. Freeman."

I waited for a reply, but he said nothing; he just studied my face as he tried to elicit the truth I so earnestly did not want to reveal. Somehow I continued, feeling I was finally admitting total defeat and relinquishing the one person who had given my life meaning, fullness, and joy in ways I'd never experienced before. "I feel completely incapable of caring for a child with such extensive and complicated medical needs, doctor. I don't have the experience or the training for it."

Dr. Freeman leaned forward very slowly, fixing his gaze on me. He obviously wanted to make sure I heard every word. "First of all, Alsie, no one is going to take this baby away from you. No one."

He paused, gazing at me hard as if willing the words to sink into my heart. Then he continued, "The time may come when we may be forced to put Stasia in an institution, but no one will ever force you to make that decision. No one, Alsie."

Again he paused, searching my eyes to make sure it was registering. I was astonished; this fear had been in me so long that I didn't know what to say. I just sat there, almost marveling that in a few words he had defused this thing that had so long filled me with dread. I began listening in earnest as he said, "Secondly, you and Brian are giving Stasia what she needs most—"

I guess I expected something so monumental at that point that I listened even more intently, as if reaching to grab this truth out of his lips and hold it like an infinitely valuable gem in my hand.

He concluded, "—and that is love."

I was amazed, dumbstruck, and for a moment chagrined. I immediately rejected his words out of hand as more of his professional kindness. It sounded like one of those standard things people say when they're trying to comfort you. I'd heard others say it multitudes of times. It was a cliché, emotional gibberish that meant little, or so I thought. I was convinced what Stasia really needed was a combination pediatrician, neurologist, orthopedic surgeon—in effect, a mini-Johns Hopkins in our home all wrapped up in me.

But love? Love was just too simple and in many ways almost insufficient because I had for so long believed this baby needed far more than that.

I said in a very small but precise voice, "You don't think they can care for her better in an institution? There are trained doctors and nurses experienced in caring for these kinds of children there."

His answer was immediate and emphatic. "No."

I just stared at him, incredulous.

He leaned forward again. "Alsie, we have done studies, extensive studies, on these children when they're removed from their homes. Their survival rate is sometimes a few weeks, sometimes a few months. When we leave them at home, though, with a loving, nurturing family, and they receive all of that love and attention they don't get in an institution because of the work load and time constraints, their survival rate never ceases to amaze us."

I remember just looking at him and saying, "That's it—love?"

It seemed to me a pat, simplistic standard. And yet Dr. Freeman was utterly serious about it in a way that I knew was not standard or pat. As I stared at him, I realized he was talking about a type of love I'd always sensed was there but had never been able to put my finger on. I was always searching for something tangible I could do to make Stasia's life comfortable and happy. That was why I felt so inadequate. But now Dr. Freeman was saying Brian and I could give Stasia something no one else could—something we were already giving her.

That was a turning-point for me, and especially in our relationship with Diana and Dr. Freeman. From then on I stopped concealing the truth from them and began telling them how things really were.

Yet, far beyond that was an even more important revelation. It was the thing I'd been searching for all my life. It was the thing I'd seen in Heidi Gutsche's family as they gathered around the table in their home to talk about God and faith and family. It was the thing Brian had given me so many times during our marriage. It was the thing Dr. Freeman and Diana had extended to both of us time and time again. It was the thing that kept Stasia alive and made her fight and keep on fighting. It was the thing that could not be bought at any price or because "you were good enough" or because "you deserved it." It was given simply because the giver wanted to give it. I would later learn it was "unconditional love," and perhaps even use technical terms like "*agape*" and "grace." It is a supernatural love that comes only from God. For the first time in a lifetime, though, my own life had meaning, real purpose. There was in me this real intangible that I could give to Stasia in a way no one else ever could or would.

Love.

Even as I write, I'm amazed that it had eluded me for so long.

Why hadn't I seen it? Why had it taken years and years of struggle before I understood any of it?

Dr. Freeman gazed at me in that room over those words, awaiting my response. In some ways it still seemed slightly ludicrous, an anti-climax.

And yet I knew in my heart that he was right and that in some monumental way once again my life had been changed for the better.

Miss Muffy

D R. FREEMAN WOULD DEMONSTRATE that brand of love to me and Brian in another way in a few weeks. After our opening "How's it going?"s, Brian spilled out the story of sleepless nights, me nodding off by the crib, the house a shambles. Dr. Freeman turned back to me and offered me another one of his thoughts on my obsessiveness about Stasia. He said, "Alsie, you cannot give and give and give to this baby. It's not healthy. She's like a bottle with a tiny little neck, and you're trying to force gallons of love down that neck. It just spills all over the place, and you end up a wreck. I want you to get out and do something fun for once. I think you ought to get a part-time job."

I began crying. "Dr. Freeman, I don't have time to get out or to get a job. I don't have time to make myself lunch because the baby needs me. I don't have time to sleep. I don't even have time to get a dog."

Dr. Freeman glanced at Brian. "A dog?"

Brian explained about Miss Ollie, my pet cocker spaniel who had died the weekend we brought Stasia home the first time. Over the months I had talked about getting another cocker, but there was never time.

Dr. Freeman peered sympathetically at me over the top of his glasses. "Do you want a cocker spaniel?" he asked.

I nodded through my tears. "It would be nice."

Dr. Freeman grabbed his prescription pad and wrote, "One cocker spaniel. Within two weeks from today." He wrote down the date. He handed it to Brian. "I won't see you again until this prescription is filled . . . Under no circumstances. And I want pictures . . . I'm not taking your word for it."

Brian was smiling. He said, "We would really like a female, doctor."

Dr. Freeman snapped the prescription back and scrawled in, "female."

Looking back, now I realize that God placed people around us who were helping us in ways we could not help ourselves. God was holding us together through all these folks who cared and gave and encouraged and encouraged and encouraged—a neurologist; his ever-faithful assistant, Diana Pillas; Dr. Adams and his family and what seemed to be armies of people from Chapelgate.

After that meeting we watched the newspapers daily and found a couple advertising a litter in Dundalk, south of Baltimore, half an hour east of Woodlawn where we lived. In less than two weeks we bought a cuddly, blonde female cocker puppy. We named her Miss Muffy, then obediently gave Dr. Freeman a Polaroid snapshot. He laughed. "So how's it feel?"

"Better," both Brian and I agreed.

Actually, though, Miss Muffy was a real handful. Housetraining seemed to go on for months. She demanded lots of attention, and visits to the vet were regular. On several occasions both of us threatened to leave the dog at the Clinic with Dr. Freeman. But I sensed a new happiness was filling our home, and it was evident to all concerned.

*

At the same time, a friend named Chris Roddy started a Bible study at our church with several nurses. She approached me about watching the baby when I needed to go out. Debbie Jackson and Patty Walters, two of the nurses, encouraged me to try it, saying they were all specially trained to work with children like Stasia. I admitted I did miss going to the local Christian Women's Luncheons. But in the end I turned them down. I knew they all had young children of their own, and I didn't feel right about "imposing."

Then one afternoon I happened to call Pauline Chisholm, the church secretary. I told her about Patty and Debbie's proposal. "It's really nice, but I can't impose like that on them."

Pauline said in her musical Scottish cadence, "If you say no to them, Alsie, remember, it will look like you're being very ungracious. They would not have volunteered if they didn't really want to do it."

I thought about it and with further questioning discovered Chris had worked out an elaborate schedule for everyone involved so that whoever took care of Stasia would have her own children watched by a second member of the group. I also realized that if Stasia ever came into any real danger, nurses like these were the best prepared to deal with it, short of a doctor, since they'd all worked in ICUs for children themselves. In the end I decided to take them up on it and began going to the luncheons once a month.

*

A definite change had subtly begun to creep into my outlook. My bitterness and anger had disappeared, or at least were not in the foreground as they had been at first. In some ways I wasn't even sure why. Part of it I knew involved my giving thanks in "little things," as I'd been doing with Stasia's smile and Miss Muffy and the friends who had gathered around us.

Then there was the constant mulling over of the "theology" of our situation. Dr. Adams's preaching on the themes of God's sovereignty, love, grace, and goodness had made an impression, even though we had not been in church as regularly as we realized we should have, due to Stasia's delicate health. Verses like Romans 8:28—"We know God causes all things to work together for good to those who love God, to those who are called according to His purpose"—popped into my mind at unexpected moments. It was one of those truths that I found difficult to believe, especially in my circumstances. And yet I had to admit I'd seen some "good" in Stasia's life, even if my little angel never lived up to any of my earlier dreams and hopes.

It wasn't any single event that caused the change; it was a subtle change of attitude that had splashed over me in little droplets here and there. The depression and anger had faded. Life was looking good again. And even if Stasia was handicapped, perhaps that was the worst of it.

God Speaks

A S THE SECOND YEAR of Stasia's life progressed, I was exhausted. My whole life had been poured into my little angel Stasia, and as Dr. Adams had suggested over a year earlier, I had run out of steam. I'd prayed for death, but it hadn't come. I'd prayed that God would take Stasia out of her pain, but it hadn't happened. I had considered suicide, but I knew I couldn't take that step, not while Stasia was still alive.

I realized I had to make a decision.

As a teenager I'd seen how my mother appeared to give up when my father died. I didn't want to live like that.

Thus, for the first time in months I began to think realistically. One thing that occurred to me was that if God Himself stood before me and explained why all this had happened to us and Stasia, it probably would never make sense to me, no matter how logical and reasonable it was to Him. No explanation would satisfy me. What would He say?

"It had to be this way."

"Why?"

"Because . . ."

Whatever "because" He might fill in, nothing would make sense. Nothing would satisfy my mercurial and probing mind. Not in this world anyway.

As I thought about it, I realized that for me this was a tremendous insight. Perhaps the reason God had not offered an explanation until now was that I wouldn't—couldn't—have accepted any He would give. It resembled the problem in the Book of Job when Satan challenged God to attack Job to see whether Job would curse Him. What if Job had known that was the basis of all his pain— a duel between God and Satan? Would that have made him feel better?

That insight alone opened a door in my mind that had until then been closed. I always asked the question, "Why?" I tended to think if I could just know why something was, I could deal with it.

Strangely, realizing now that God could never give me a clear and comforting explanation set me free. I no longer sought to "figure it all out." There were only two choices: acceptance or suicide. I'd ruled out the latter.

And that brought me to the even bigger issue: acceptance. Could I just accept my situation as from the hand of God? Could I see it as good and worthwhile even if I did not understand why it had all happened? Could I in a sense embrace it gladly, take it into my arms, and say "Thanks," knowing it was from the heart and mind of a loving, wise, all-knowing Heavenly Father? I knew it had to be more than resigned acceptance, like the person who bows in defeat to his fate and places his neck on the chopping block. No, real acceptance involved much more—a joyous embracing of the trial and suffering, realizing that I wouldn't try to circumvent it, go around it or above it or under it. No, I would have to walk straight through this tragedy with head up and heart soaring, believing that God had somehow sent it to me because He loved me.

To me, this was a monumental contradiction and a dilemma.

Then something else happened.

One afternoon near the end of the summer of 1988, I sat alone in the family room with Stasia. I gazed out at the sunshine through the sliding glass doors. It was a sparkling, sun-splashy day, the kind

I always loved and craved. I thought about taking Stasia for a walk, but knowing how easily she contracted bronchitis or an infection, I decided against it. Faintly, in the background, I noticed myself humming one more time "Brahms' Lullaby."

And then with sudden clarity and the cool, visual effect of stark reality, a drama began playing itself out before my eyes. In my mind's eye suddenly there was a picture, a scene. Whether it actually appeared and would have seen by someone else, had they been present, I don't know. But for me it was as real as the child in my arms.

God seemed to be sitting on a throne holding court. Then, hearing a sudden call, a multitude of childish souls pranced into the throne room in happy ranks, whispering and laughing in their childish voices. My heart was booming.

They all sat down before God. He said, "I have an important job for someone. I need a volunteer."

A multitude of tiny hands flew up, and the children cried for Him to pick them, just like children do when they're in kindergarten or first grade. They were all smiling, all equally sincere and emphatic in their desires. I didn't know whether I was dreaming, asleep, or having a vision, but I could not take my eyes off what I was seeing.

God went on, "There are two special people who have a long way to go, special things to learn. I need someone . . ."

All the little hands went up again.

"It's not easy down there," He said. "It's very hard. People are fragile. When they're scared, they do bad things to little people. Sometimes they hurt you. But I still need someone . . ."

Fewer hands were going up, but many voices called to Him. "Me." "Me." "Me."

The majestic Presence went on, "Sometimes they put you in an institution for a long time. I need someone who will be ready to deal with that."

Even fewer hands went up.

"They might get so angry and bitter that they strike you or say harsh things to you or forget you and wish you had never existed."

Only a few hands were up now. One of the children asked, "What's the good part?"

"The good part is that there's the chance," God intoned, "that these people whom I love will see this through. They'll determine to do their best even in the midst of a horrible situation. They'll love you and keep on loving you no matter what comes. And when they do, they'll experience a joy and an insight that is beyond their world. There's the potential for a lot of bad and a lot of hurt, but also for a joy that will last forever."

At that point only one hand was up. In my mind's eye I saw the face. It was little Stasia.

My mouth dropped in shock, and instantly the picture faded, leaving me in a stunned, misty silence. I looked at Stasia and saw that the tiny girl was asleep

For the next few hours I debated back and forth. What had happened? Was it real? Would God really speak to me like that? Could Stasia have been sent? Was she an "angel in disguise"? Or was this all some theological hallucination, born of lack of sleep, weariness, and inattentiveness to my own health?

After hours of meditation I didn't know what to think. I am not one given to visions and dreams. Like my husband, I just want the facts, please. I'd never undergone a mystical or "religious experience," never had an emotional "born-again" episode like some have described. Thus the whole experience threw me. Would people think I was crazy if I told them?

I concluded that regardless of the reality of the vision, or whatever it was, a truth had lodged in my soul: What if Stasia in some divine sense had been "sent" to us, to me and Brian, for a purpose we could never fully understand, but for reasons that God planned to use for good, reasons God knew would leave us with an eternal joy? What if this was all part of a majestic sovereign plan, as I'd heard Dr. Adams and other preachers speak about? I knew God hadn't caused bad in order to bring about good. But I thought of it this way: despite the evils of a fallen world, He Himself can turn even tragedies and defeats into joy and peace in the lives of those He loves. Was that it? Was that the secret He was trying to tell me?

This was a foreign concept to me, something I'd never quite understood, and certainly never believed.

But what if?

That night I told Brian about it when he came home. He didn't want to at the time, but he couldn't help it—he laughed. "I think you've been cooped up in this house too long!"

"But don't you see?" I insisted. "What if Stasia somehow came here for a purpose? What if God sent her and it all does have a purpose—for us, for her, for everyone? What if it can be used for good?"

"You're crazy!" Brian said. His own frustration still raged within, and when some religious-sounding phrase like this was fired at him, it all came out. "This can never be for good!" he said quietly, sounding defeated.

Stilling myself, a hard thing to do for one as determined as me to convince others of my point of view, I stopped and decided to pray about it on my own. "All right, if this thing is of God, then I'm going to pursue it. I'm going to find out."

That night before bed, when Brian was somewhere else in the house, I knelt and prayed. "Okay, God, I think this stinks. I can't imagine that anything good can come from Stasia's condition. But You've said in Your Word that You 'work all things together for good for those who love God.' I'm willing to accept that. But You've got to show me, and You've got to show me soon. I can't wait around until ten years from now to understand at least part of it. I need to know if there's something good in all this, because all I can see is the bad. If You will do that, I'll see it through."

This was for me the greatest turning-point of my life with Stasia, and also the end of a process which I now believe sealed my conversion to faith in Christ. For years I'd fought an inner battle with God about His existence, His goodness, His love, His presence. If things were good, I believed. But if things went sour, God was a figment of others' imaginations.

I shuffled the images in my mind of my friend Heidi Gutsche in high school, my experiences in various churches, the loving people at Chapelgate, the many Christian friends I'd made, and threw it all against the difficulties Stasia had faced. How did a person put it all together?

I still wasn't sure. I sensed I had begun a relationship with Him that touched me at the deepest places.

Over the next few weeks I mulled my "vision" over and over in my mind. I wasn't sure I understood the theology of it, but I knew this time I had changed dramatically. I was beginning to think there was a purpose in Stasia's life. Could something good come from all this pain?

For the first time, I set my heart on finding out what.

Telling the Story

LATER THAT MONTH Stasia seemed to improve. Dr. Freeman reiterated, "Children like this thrive in a home setting. You're giving her the most important thing she needs—love. The reason she's still alive is because you love her."

The summer and fall of her second year of life already looked far better than the first, both for us and for Stasia. I again became convinced we would beat this handicap, no matter how unchangeable Dr. Freeman said it was; I was sure all would be well.

As the weeks burned by, I found new joy in Stasia's health. I began to realize how absolutely dependent my little angel was on me. An earlier train of thought, honed against my tendency to think in broad theological terms, developed within me. It appeared that through Stasia God was teaching me a powerful lesson about unconditional love and grace that I'd never quite understood before.

As I mentioned before, my upbringing led me to the conviction that obedience was rewarded and disobedience was profoundly punished. I'd always seen God in the same terms. I'd heard and known nothing of Biblical love, *agape*, unconditional, "keeps on giving" love, the kind that God demonstrated in Jesus Christ. Such love just appeared impossible to me.

But in Stasia I saw something entirely different. It occurred to me at first that I had in my arms every mother's dream. While a sixteen-year-old daughter might be killed by a drunk driver, or a thirty-five-year-old son could be struck down with cancer, I would never feel that sense of separation. Stasia would be a baby for the rest of her life, utterly dependent, utterly mine. She would never reach an age where she rejected her mother in any way. My baby would always be a baby, innocent, simple, returning in a smile or a coo all that she possessed of a loving response.

Frequently I noticed how some parents would push their children around, yelling at them, embarrassing them. I'd see mothers jamming pacifiers into little babies' mouths after they had fallen to the floor. A sense of anger welled up inside me, but also of empathy. I suddenly wanted to embrace those moms and dads and cry, "Do you know how blessed you are that your child can even hold a pacifier? Do you realize what you have—a healthy child?"

But above all, I saw that no matter how much Brian and I believed that Stasia understood who we were and how we cared about her, Stasia would never know that gift in the same way an older, normal child would. I would never hear an "I love you, Mommy" from Stasia's lips.

Strangely, that no longer troubled me. Only months before, that problem had burned me up with outrage at God and the world, but now there was something different—a calm, peace.

Acceptance.

That was what it had come to. I actually accepted the situation just as I had envisioned weeks before. There were still unanswered questions, there was more pain to come, but I'd accepted it in a way I never had been able to before.

I was sure our situation would never change for the better in some miraculous way, but I was no longer fighting it, hating it, cursing it. I had come to see it as coming from the hand of a loving God who chose to give us a gift He gave few others. This was a marvelous truth, and it stirred in me a depth of gratitude that I wished I could put into words.

But there was another side to it, the "unconditional," grace side that I was hearing in Bible studies and reading in the Scriptures that had so often made me squirm in days past. I was learning to give love in a whole new way. For so long I'd seen love as, You give me this, and I'll give you that. But with Stasia there was little, if any, thanks, love, or return offered.

Yes, I had seen the "little things" of Stasia's nature and personality and had come to appreciate them. The morning "hah" and the July 4th smile and the bath were all wonderful and worthwhile responses. But they were really so few and so far between. I realized I probably would never know that Dr. Freeman wasn't right: whether they were just "automatic" responses, gas, or just the normal expression of pleasure having nothing to do with Brian and me as people, as parents.

This was a difficult idea to get into my head. What it came down to was that I knew I accepted and loved Stasia not because of her "potential" or her personality or her gifts or anything else she had or did. I accepted her because she was God's gift, a valuable human being. I could accept Stasia as she was, and I could love her because of what she was.

At times I wondered if I had truly gone to that limit. But then I saw how we had laid it all out before Stasia's birth. Brian and I had planned out schools and lessons and sports and places to go; indeed, every stage of Stasia's life had been arranged. Almost laughing, we realized we were prime candidates for autocracy in parenting.

Then we'd had to give it all up in the face of Stasia's handicaps and increasing problems. That led to the anger and bitterness.

But with acceptance came a change for the better, a chance to really love someone unconditionally and not force our child to go our way. It occurred to me that was part of the reason Stasia was born into our family. Diana often said she believed that God simply wanted to change me and Brian for the better.

This turning-point was confirmed one day in a store when I

crossed paths with a woman I hadn't seen since I'd been pregnant. We'd both been pregnant at the same time and had talked in the doctor's office about our hopes and plans for our soon-to-be-born babies. But we had lost touch since our respective maternities.

Naturally she asked me how it had all turned out. I began to tell the story of Stasia, her handicaps, the trauma, the difficulties. As I spoke, though, I noticed the changes in her facial expression, something that always occurred when I told people about Stasia. First, there was disbelief, then pain, and finally pity. I had always liked the pity, thinking it was my "due" in view of what I and Stasia were going through. For a long time I had wanted the "pity parties." I savored the sensation of knowing that people "hurt for me" and "felt sorry for me."

But this time I realized that was not what I wanted at all.

What I wanted people to see was what a wonderful gift this child was to me and Brian, a child sent from God. I wanted them to know how greatly Stasia had changed me, how this little powerless person had made me see things I'd never thought about before: unconditional love, grace, acceptance, embracing a trial as from the loving hand of God.

People seemed to be so sorry that Stasia really didn't have "much of a life." And that was true. But Stasia did have a purpose. I so wanted people to see that. Stasia was not some horrible fluke of fate or some dreadful accident. She was rather the best thing that ever happened to us, to me and Brian, to my whole family. Stasia had come into this world poorly equipped to handle life's storms and trials. But that was because she was of a spirit not of this world. She was filled with something marvelous that you see now and then in such special people. They're firmly planted on earth, but their hearts and actions point you to Heaven.

True, Stasia would never walk, talk, sit up, or take care of herself. She wouldn't go to college or raise a family or become president of Citicorp. But God was merciful. She'd also never know what it was like to be lied to or betrayed or hurt by a friend.

Everyone had something to give. Everyone played a role in God's magnificent drama, and Stasia had played hers to Oscar perfection.

As I continued to talk, and as my friend didn't seem to understand what I was saying, I thought of the countless people who had spoken to me about Stasia's emotional and spiritual impact on them. How she touched the heart and soul. How her occasional glimmer of a smile, her dark blue, unfocused eyes, her calmness—how each of those facets of her nature taught others what was truly important in life—that we are all dependent on One greater than ourselves. Stasia seemed to exude a sense of the value of life, of knowing God, of what it is He wants of us. Stasia had taught me about trust, absolute and unquestioning trust, about total dependence and faith in God.

As I talked, those were the realities I wanted to get across to my friend. But when it seemed all my friend could muster was that same pity I'd seen so often before, I told myself not to force it. It didn't matter if I couldn't convey what Stasia had done. Stasia had changed me, and I knew it. That was enough.

The OG Tube

B Y THE END OF THE SUMMER OF 1988, it was clear that Stasia was not gaining weight significantly. It was taking me longer and longer to feed her. Without the weight, she was extremely susceptible to illness and dehydration. It was critical for us get Stasia up to normal weight and keep her properly nourished simply to maintain what health she had.

Thus, one of the real breakthroughs was a method of feeding that Dr. Freeman recommended at that time, something called an OG Tube (Oral-Gastric). Actually, there were two types—an NG Tube (Nasogastric) and the OG. Because Stasia was so vulnerable to sinus infections, we chose the OG method over the NG. In effect, this method of feeding allowed us to directly supply food to her stomach through a tube inserted in her mouth and down her esophagus.

We learned how to place the tube in Stasia's throat and guide it down her esophagus to her stomach. We were taught to ensure that the tube had landed in her stomach and not her lungs by holding a stethoscope to her abdomen and forcing a swallow of air down the tube. If there was a "pop," then it was in properly. This apparatus made it possible for Stasia to digest much larger quantities of food and to gain weight rapidly and consistently.

However, this was just a temporary arrangement. Our goal was a complete gastrostomy in which a permanent hole would be created in her abdomen and a tube inserted for more direct and efficient feeding. The OG method, while helpful, was not a long-term solution. It was uncomfortable and risky because of the possibility of accidentally guiding the tube into her lungs and not knowing it until she suffocated. Our doctors said the OG tube would enable her to gain the weight necessary for the gastrostomy operation.

The OG tube worked well. Stasia consumed normal quantities of formula. She gained weight. It rarely took more than twenty minutes to a half hour to feed her. Suddenly I had far more time to care for Stasia's other needs and to simply hold her and love her. Brian and I also were rewarded with greater freedom to spend time with one another.

But in another sense I felt defeated and a bit depressed. The one thing that I could always count on in terms of a response from Stasia was the feeding. Hard as it was sitting for two or three hours straight trying to get her to take an ounce or two of formula and baby food, it was still an uplifting, rewarding, intimate time for us. I could see her responses. Her little mouth crinkling, her eyes showing expression—all of that had been so important to me. It was the one time Stasia "expressed" herself on a daily basis. It was the one time I felt "normal" and that I was doing something all mothers do. Taking all that away with the OG Tube left me feeling defeated and somehow detached from Stasia in a way I didn't like and struggled with for several months.

Still, her health improved, and for that I was thankful. Both Brian and I believed Stasia was starting on a period of health that could be sustained if a few more problems were solved.

"A few more problems," though, was an understatement. There was the spinal condition; the muscle contractures; the seizures; the difficulties with feeding, choking, and her sinuses; the serious concerns about weight, growth, digestion, and sleep patterns. In addition, Stasia was regularly taking several powerful medications that were rarely administered to children in such doses singly let alone in the combinations and potencies she was receiving.

However, beyond all this in my own mind was Stasia's scoliosis—the abnormal curvature of her spine and the malformed vertebrae that made her so uncomfortable. We had learned that an operation could be performed through which the doctors would fuse the damaged bones, insert a metal rod, and ensure normal curvature. This would only work, however, if Stasia's problem was physical; if it was neurological, such a procedure could be deadly because eventually the spine would twist back out of shape, and the rod would break off and possibly kill her.

In my mind, though, I saw this as the only hope on the horizon. Before all these problems had appeared—the seizures, the scoliosis, the contractures—Stasia had actually been shimmying around in the crib, craning her neck and looking about, and appearing to try to turn over. Moreover, Dr. Sponseller, our orthopedic specialist, told us that the curvature of Stasia's spine put pressure on her lungs. This made pneumonia a greater danger. I believed the back operation could possibly prolong her life. And this to me was paramount. I thought if we could just get Stasia's spine corrected, everything would be set back on course, and the handicaps would disappear.

The gastrostomy was scheduled for early November 1988. I believed that if Stasia fared well through this, then we could move on to correcting the scoliosis. However, as November drew near, Dr. Freeman was not as optimistic about the back surgery as I was. He intimated a number of times that it might not work. This soon moved on to a stronger conviction that it *would* not work. Tunneler of vision that I am, I did not hear any of this. I merely focused on the goal—the gastrostomy and then the back operation; after that, all would be well. That was all that mattered.

✱

A final blow came shortly before the gastrostomy. All through the fall I thought about the back surgery. That had to be the answer. If the spine problem was corrected, Stasia would go back to the way she had been just before the seizures started. We'd be back on track. She would develop normally. I went to our next appointment with a determination to convince Dr. Freeman this was all that was needed.

We sat down in the little conference room, with Diana near the door; Brian and I sat in the middle with Stasia in our little baby carrier. Dr. Freeman sat, as always, in his desk chair on wheels next to the desk. We talked about how things were going, and finally I brought up the back operation.

Though we'd discussed it several times before and he'd been moderately negative about it, this time Dr. Freeman dismissed it out of hand as diagnostically unfeasible. It would not produce the results we wanted. But I pressed him, making sure I didn't mention my thoughts about getting Stasia "back on track." I knew Dr. Freeman would find that train of thought preposterous.

Dr. Freeman raised his eyebrows in surprise and consternation. Then he said, "Alsie, why do you want this so much? Why are you pushing this?"

I stammered something about wanting to see Stasia get better, be more comfortable. He said, "Do you understand what this operation is all about?"

"Sure," I said, unsure of where all this was going, but just as determined to convince him it was right.

"No, you don't," he said with sudden force. "Let me tell you." He began to spell out the details of what would be done. The three irregularly shaped vertebrae in Stasia's back would be removed, and her spine would be fused together at those points. Next, a steel rod would be attached to her spine with wires. Finally, she would be sewn up and put into a body cast. The recovery period would be months, perhaps as long as a year. It was a very painful, very expensive operation, and it might not work because if the problem was neurological, eventually the spine would twist again and break from the rod, killing her. Dr. Freeman said, "If she lives three years, Alsie, that one year is a third of her life. Imagine if you lived ninety years and thirty years of it was in recovery from a back operation. Think of what that would mean for Stasia!"

His intensity unnerved me, but I plunged on, still careful not to tell him what was at the bottom of my insistence. "But, Dr. Freeman, she'd be happier and not be in the pain she's in now."

"Her pain would be greater. And there would still be the long recovery period—one third of her life!"

"But she'd be more comfortable—I know it."

"Maybe," he said. "But that's not for sure, and there's still the recovery third of her life, Alsie. A third of it."

As he shot down my arguments, I felt my inner compass go awry and a terrible hysteria burning in my mind. "But, Dr. Freeman," I tried to say, "if she has her back corrected and I can put her back on her stomach . . ."

"It won't *stay* corrected, Alsie. The problem is not physiological but neurological. And brain cells do not replicate. Once they die, they're gone forever. Think . . ." Dr. Freeman was closer, staring at me, pushing, trying to get me to see what was going on.

"But if she can get back on her stomach—" I was crying now, my little girl at my feet. Everything seemed to be crumbling inside.

Dr. Freeman said, "This is not the NICU, Alsie. You go crazy if Stasia has a little black mark on her face. The pain would be tremendous, constant, overwhelming. Can you live with that?"

"But she has to be made right!" I said. "It will do it . . . I know it."

Dr. Freeman moved forward on the little chair. "The operation is not going to make it right," he said. "Stasia might make it through the operation, but she might not survive the recovery and the Pediatric Intensive Care Unit. Do you understand that?"

He had annihilated every argument and with it all the hope I'd had. I became hysterical, weeping into my hands and saying, "Why can't you just fix it? Please just fix it!"

Dr. Freeman put his hands on mine very gently, and as I looked up into his sad, weary eyes I said, "You're so smart . . . such a great doctor . . . Why can't you fix this?"

The room was very quiet. Finally Dr. Freeman said, "Alsie, if there was one patient in my whole career, one baby I could help and no one else, from the bottom of my heart, it would be Stasia." He looked deeply into my eyes and said, "But I can't do that, Alsie. It cannot be done. It is not in my power."

✳

We moved closer to the gastrostomy operation, my emotions a tumble of worry, fear, and a deep sense of defeat. But I still held out for the back operation, even though Dr. Freeman had been so adamant that it wouldn't work. Even as we left that afternoon, I did not feel the situation had ended. Dr. Freeman had not completely closed the door.

In early November we took Stasia to Johns Hopkins for the gastrostomy.

This particular operation had provoked tremendous tension in all of the medical people involved. Stasia was still small for a surgery of this kind. At one and a half, she weighed less than ten pounds. In her blankets in the baby carriage, she looked tiny. People still asked when she'd been born, as if it had been yesterday.

We went in on a Sunday night. After Stasia was admitted, one of the first chores necessary was starting an IV and taking blood. This remained a problem throughout her life, and at only ten pounds it was an extremely difficult maneuver to pull off. A resident and several nurses took her into a treatment room. I sat down with Stasia, holding her hand and singing "Brahms' Lullaby," trying to calm her so she would keep still. Brian helped also, capping off the tiny vials of blood or just providing support. It was not normal procedure to let parents into a treatment room, but we were both well-established as helpful to the process, and by this time no one tried to prevent us from assisting.

It seemed like forever. No one could find a vein. Stasia did not understand what was going on and periodically became agitated. Sweat streamed off everyone's face, and the tension mounted.

Strangely, Dr. Marshall Stone, the surgeon who would perform the gastrostomy, happened to be on the floor that night. Dr. Stone is a young man, in his mid-forties, very friendly and down to earth. Both Brian and I immediately liked him. He always wears a sheriff's badge that says, "Marshall Stone" and uses it to encourage children to talk and have some fun with him. He stopped by the room and saw us all working on Stasia. Realizing we were having difficulty, he volunteered, "It's been a long time since I started an IV, but let me give it a try."

Everyone was a little taken aback. Johns Hopkins has an IV Team whose job is to go around the hospital starting IVs when and where necessary. Because it was the weekend, they weren't available. I was surprised in particular because I'd picked up that many doctors, especially a top pediatric surgeon, considered things like this "beneath them," akin to having to change a bedpan. But Dr. Stone plunged in, and in a matter of seconds he had a professional, flawless IV in place. He broke into a great grin and quipped, "I've still got the touch!"

Afterwards one of the nurses said to me, "I've never seen a surgeon put in an IV! That was amazing."

The next day was the operation. Stasia was wheeled down to the operating room on her bed. Brian remained outside, but I went in with Stasia to help calm her with the "Lullaby." Inside, all the doctors seemed tense and fearful about performing the surgery. The biggest worry was getting Stasia off the respirator after the operation. Would she start breathing on her own again after she was taken off? The biggest fear, of course, was that Stasia wouldn't survive the operation. Determining the proper levels of anesthesia presented tremendous difficulties, and three anesthesiologists were present.

One of the peculiarities about Stasia's condition was her rare smiles. On July 4 she'd smiled all day. But since then, no one had witnessed one in months. She also had great trouble focusing her electric blue eyes. Her pupils always looked dilated, full of a kind of inner but distant excitement, eyes that, as some commented, "seemed to know far more than she told."

I sat in a rocker holding Stasia as she slept. Finally she was gently laid on the operating table. We were surrounded by doctors and nurses as she lay small and vulnerable on the table.

I could see the concern on the faces of the three anesthesiologists, but there was also a great deal of compassion as they peered down at our tiny little daughter. How small and fragile she looked on that large table.

One of the doctors suddenly said, "She's cold. Bring a warm blanket."

As everyone peered anxiously at this tiny little slip of a child, that precious grin with all of its sweetness and innocence began to spread slowly from ear to ear, as if to say, "Everything is going to be all right."

That sweet smile continued to radiate out toward everyone. The doctor said, "Look at that grin . . . Look at that grin!" Everyone seemed to visibly relax.

It was a holy moment, another one of those turning-points that both Brian and I came to treasure as an unfathomable gift God was bestowing upon us all through this angelic child.

I left as everything was secured, and the operation proceeded. In the waiting room we prayed and talked, hoping soon we would hear all was well. Dr. Stone finally came out and told us, "Everything is fine. The operation is a success. She'll be coming out soon and be sent up to the PICU."

We thanked him, sending silent prayers of thanks up to God for giving us a little more time.

*

But a half hour later Stasia was wheeled out. Both of us stared, aghast. Her eyes were black as if someone had punched her. She looked frail and helpless and so tiny on the gurney. Even the aftermath of the hernia operation over a year ago had been nothing like this. We followed them up to the PICU, but they wouldn't let us in.

Brian and I waited outside. Diana came by, and I complained that they weren't letting us see her. She asked how long we'd been out there—it had been ten or twenty minutes—and Diana just shook her head, saying, "Oh, come on, will you two get serious? They've got a lot of work to do. You'll see her!"

I bit my tongue and waited anxiously with Brian.

About an hour later we were admitted. The PICU was a real shock to both of us. There were two patients to each room, with one full-time nurse for both. It was far more intensive than the NICU, and clearly far more serious. There were monitors, respirators, trays and trays of tools and medications, and an endless stream of nurses moving very quickly from place to place. The nurse in Stasia's room was a whirlwind of motion, checking monitors, administering medication, keeping doctors informed. Suddenly the reality of the words "intensive care" sunk in.

Stasia looked terrible. She had a large tube down her throat to assist her in breathing. Her breathing was laborious. Her eyes were puffy and black, her face and body mottled and bruised. It seemed as if wires and IVs and monitors and lines in every direction were connected to her body. When Stasia did awake, she was clearly in distress. She tried to cry, but because of the tube in her throat, the sound was muffled and even more wrenching than usual. In all our one and a half years together, nothing had been this bad.

That night we stayed several hours later than normal visiting hours. Brian sat out in the hall taking a break. At night it was extremely quiet, the halls lit only by what was barely necessary, so the patients could sleep. Then two doors down from Stasia's room, one of the children, a little girl, died. Immediately terrible wrenching wails broke the quiet as the girl's mother witnessed her child's death. Moments later the grandfather stepped out of the room, and Brian looked up at him. The man looked stunned, holding on to the wall to steady himself, as if someone had just shot him in the stomach.

That vision became imprinted on Brian's mind, something I wouldn't know about for many months. He knew, though, that this was what he and I were coming to with Stasia. The picture of his little girl dying like that, hooked up to a multitude of machines, with medical people hovering about and devastated parents being shoved off into a corner, was something he knew he could not allow to happen. It would later become the defining point of his own faith.

At the time, though, I was only thinking of how to make Stasia more comfortable and to help her endure this. But for Brian a decision had come. He told me later that when he saw Stasia in the PICU like this and witnessed the results of the death of the little girl down the hall, he resolved that the back operation would not take place. The next day he told Dr. Freeman he did not want Stasia to go through it. Dr. Freeman answered, "I agree. How do we tell Alsie?"

Later they would find a way to break the news. But for the moment all my attention was focused on getting Stasia out of the PICU with no complications and back home.

Another Word of Encouragement

STASIA WAS IN THE PICU just over twenty-four hours. The tube in her throat was removed early the following morning, and she breathed on her own satisfactorily. They took her to the Pediatric Surgery floor where she stayed for the next ten days. When we finally took her home, we had less than a week before we were scheduled to move to our new home in Columbia, Maryland.

While still at the old house, I discovered blood in the baby's diaper when I changed her. I knew that was serious enough to warrant leaving for Hopkins immediately.

First, I took Stasia in to see Dr. Scott Strahlmann, our pediatrician. He made the arrangements to have Stasia readmitted to Johns Hopkins that day. I drove out to Columbia and found Brian in front of our new house waiting for the moving van. I told him, "I'm on my way to Hopkins. Come as soon as you can."

I sped to Johns Hopkins, a seventeen-minute steeplechase of a ride from Columbia. I spent hours in the emergency room as doctors worked on Stasia. When she was finally admitted to the hospital in stable condition, I stayed by her side and fell asleep that night in an extra bed. About 3 A.M. I was awakened by the beeping of the IV alarm. A nurse arrived, and as I stood to assist her, everything seemed to go blurry, I couldn't seem to move my foot out to balance myself, and I collapsed back onto the bed, unconscious.

Moments later the nurse hovered over me, asking me if I was all right. I said, "I guess so."

Everyone knew about my almost fanatical attention to Stasia to the detriment of my own health. She immediately asked, "When was the last time you ate?"

I knew this was serious, but I finally said, "I don't remember."

"Uh-huh." She told me to sit down and not move. She left, then returned a few minutes later with orange juice laced with sugar. Without saying any more about it, she noted everything in her report, even though I did not know that at the time.

The next morning, Saturday, I awoke early, still in Stasia's room. Upon opening my eyes, I noticed a pair of men's shoes on the other side of Stasia's crib. Looking up, my heart sank. It was Dr. Freeman.

I thought if I could just jump up and start talking, I could dance my way out of this one. I sat up and as cheerfully as possible said, "Good morning, Dr. Freeman. How's my little Stasia doing?"

With a little smile on his face, Dr. Freeman stared me down. "I understand we had a little excitement last night."

I was still bent on bluffing my way out of the situation, and I blustered, "Well, you know her veins are so small, and they don't hold the IV well and . . ."

"That's not what I mean. I understand you passed out last night."

"How do you know about that?"

"The nurse wrote it in her report."

"I can't believe she would betray me like that!"

Dr. Freeman said evenly, "My nurses are trained to report everything that happens on this floor."

I cringed, fearing he'd really ban me from the floor this time.

"Listen," Dr. Freeman said in a deep, commanding voice, "if you don't take care of yourself, and that means eating and sleeping, you're not going to do the baby any good."

"But, Dr. Freeman, I . . ."

"I've written orders to the nurses that you are to eat breakfast and then be off this floor and go home and sleep, and you are not allowed back for a minimum of three hours."

"But, Dr. Freeman, there's no one to watch Stasia."

Dr. Freeman's smile faded instantly. "Alsie, we spend a great deal of time and money to train our doctors and nurses here at Johns Hopkins. I can assure you they are well-qualified to take excellent care of Stasia."

I knew I was beaten, but I tried one more ploy. "But, Dr. Freeman, they don't know her. They can't look into her eyes and know what she needs; they don't understand the noises she makes and what they mean. Suppose Stasia needs me?"

With an abrupt sigh, Dr. Freeman said, "Okay, when will Brian be here?" Even he knew when he was tangling with a crazed mom.

"About 7:30 with breakfast, and then the grandmothers will be here around 9:30."

"Okay. When the grandmas arrive, you are to leave the floor and not come back until tonight. And be sure to eat breakfast."

I looked demurely at my hands, then back into his stern eyes. "Thanks, Dr. Freeman."

"I'm serious," he said with sudden intensity. "If you don't leave, the nurses are to call me at home, and I will instruct Security to escort you out of this hospital."

"I love you, Dr. Freeman."

"Then do what I say."

After Brian arrived with breakfast, the nurse came back in and asked, "Did you have breakfast, Alsie?"

"Yes," I said happily.

The nurse sighed and looked sheepish, then added, "I'm sorry, but I'm under orders to see the empty plates."

Brian laughed. "Dr. Freeman doesn't miss a beat."

It was then that Brian and I decided on a routine. I would go home at night about eleven o'clock so I could sleep, and Brian would stay at the hospital sleeping next to the baby's crib. I would bring a fresh change of clothes for Brian in the morning. He would shower there and shave and then go to work. About 5:30 he'd rejoin me and we'd spend the rest of the evening together with Stasia until I left between 11 and 12 P.M.

New Insights

NOW HAVING A LITTLE TIME to think and pray about all the new ideas that were filling my mind, I found myself repeatedly meditating on Romans 8:28. The picture of God "working all things for good" for people like me, Brian, and Stasia seemed incredible, and yet I had begun to believe it was true.

The text seemed to say that while evil is rampant in this world, and though God does not terminate it in most cases, He does do something else: He works around it, over it, under it. He allows the harsh jabs and thrusts of sin to go on, but at the same time He always strips it of its ultimate destructive power. He allows evil, and He allows evil to at times do its worst; but always, always, He preserves His people so that something good springs from sin's poisonous soil.

For me, this was a balancing point between the "do this, get that" theology of my youth and other ideas of "grinning and bearing" that I learned later. No, I wasn't a victim, nor was Stasia. Somehow Stasia had been destined for her role in our lives. God had planned it carefully from all eternity, and though He knew it would be painful for everyone concerned, He "meant it for good," just as Joseph had explained to his brothers in the fiftieth chapter of Genesis when they were afraid he would retaliate for their selling him into slavery. Moreover, I began to think God could and would turn all our pain into a source of peace and joy that produces genuine gratitude despite the difficulties.

During this time, Dr. Lane Adams sent us Christopher de Vinck's book, *The Power of the Powerless* (New York: Doubleday, 1988). This book told the story of de Vinck's brother Oliver, a severely handicapped boy who lived thirty-two years without ever speaking or caring for himself in any way. The anecdote that particularly struck us was early in the book, when de Vinck, an English teacher, told his students about Helen Keller in the play *The Miracle Worker*. One of the students raised his hand during the lecture and said, "Oh, Mr. de Vinck, you mean Oliver was a vegetable." De Vinck stammered for a moment and finally replied, "Well, I guess you could call him a vegetable. I called him Oliver, my brother. You would have loved him" (p. 9). Chris revealed that Oliver had in his powerlessness changed the world in which we live, from the millions of people who read the story in *Reader's Digest* and elsewhere, to President Reagan.

To both Brian and me this was an amazing affirmation. Just as Chris de Vinck had seen value and worth in Oliver, we both saw the same thing in Stasia. Some might call her a vegetable, but we called her Stasia, our little angel, our beloved daughter.

More than that, we could see there were other families in the world who experienced the same heartbreaks as we had, and they had emerged joyous, glad to have taken part in a severely handicapped child's journey. We gave copies of the book to Dr. Freeman and Diana. Dr. Freeman later told us it was the best book on the subject he'd ever read, and he wanted more copies; he wanted to suggest it as good reading for his students.

What was most difficult for me, though, was conveying these thoughts to Brian. While I was experiencing a spiritual rejuvenation, Brian remained angry and solemn, convinced that God would never do anything to change our situation dramatically. He couldn't understand my turnaround, and this new joy I seemed to be gushing all over the place. Our relationship continued to deteriorate. I was wrapped up in taking care of the baby, feeling that Stasia would not be with us that much longer. I believed it was all right to "put Brian on hold" while I gave 100 percent to Stasia. Brian, though, resented this and withdrew deeper into a hostile silence.

One thing, though, I knew that even Brian couldn't deny was the impact Stasia was having on others.

One evening I invited our friend Bill Morris to dinner. It would be the first time in Stasia's life that we had someone other than family over for an intimate social occasion. Bill had been a bachelor a long time. Then in his thirties he married, and soon his much younger wife gave him a little boy. Less than a year later he was caught in the midst of a nasty divorce.

People describe Bill as gregarious, with a refreshing curiosity and playfulness about the world. But everyone could see his divorce was tearing him apart. It appeared that their infant son was caught in the middle, and Bill was agonizing over the whole situation.

Both Brian and I were concerned how Bill would react to a severely handicapped child. We both knew he had been hurt deeply by his divorce and the custody battle, and we simply wanted to extend a friendly hand. Above all, neither of us wanted him to feel pressured to "put on a happy face" around Stasia. So I decided to make it as easy on him as I could. I planned the whole day so that Stasia could remain in the background if necessary and not put Bill on the spot.

Normally I would give Stasia a sedative for a few hours of rest during the day. Because Stasia never kept any sort of schedule, it was impossible to organize anything outside the home around her. The problem was that when Stasia was awake, I always had to give her my undivided attention. I knew that wouldn't work with guests. So I gave Stasia a sedative at 10 in the morning, hoping she'd sleep for a few hours, awaken, eat, and then sleep again in the early evening after Bill arrived. I hoped she would be asleep while Bill was there, thus creating a much more social occasion.

Stasia, however, had not been informed of the details of my plan. Perhaps she was unhappy that her concerns weren't taken into consideration. Or maybe an angel touched her that evening. Whatever it was, she slept from 10 until 6 in the evening, and when Bill arrived at 6:30 she was as awake as a chickadee at day-break waiting for her breakfast. Bill promptly informed both of us of how depressed he was. I felt terribly guilty, glancing at Brian and hoping he could take over. Then I excused myself, determined to make the best of it.

I sat down in the rocker with Stasia in my arms and began the routine, now feeding her regularly with the feed pump into her Gastro-Tube. I couldn't get dinner ready now, so Brian fumbled around in the kitchen, but I already imagined disaster was closing in. However, Bill ambled into the family room and, not being par-ticularly hungry, took a seat on the sofa and began watching me and the baby with interest. Brian and I both tried to talk to him, but with me concentrating on Stasia and Brian jumping up and down with little chores related to the feeding, Bill didn't get a lot of TLC.

A few minutes into the feeding, though, Bill got off the sofa and walked over to our seat. He knelt at my feet, hovering just over Stasia's face, and watched, a look of obvious childish fascination on his face. I could see he was literally enthralled with Stasia—not with the feeding, but with the child herself.

He began talking about her. "I've never seen anyone like her. She's so at peace. She's like an angel. She's . . . She's . . . She's . . ." Our amazing Stasia made him feel love for everyone. That little angelic girl was the epitome of innocence and all that was good in the world.

Bill couldn't stop staring. Though he was still kneeling, his emo-tions were floating six feet off the ground.

When he'd first arrived, he talked about nothing but how the divorce had torn the whole family apart and how both he and his wife had been using their child to hurt one another. But over the next three hours, spent gazing at and talking about Stasia, he began to say, "None of that matters anymore. Watching you all with the baby and how you interact with her . . . it's the most amazing thing I've ever seen."

When he left that night, he was happy, excited, and overflowing with a joy neither Brian nor I could explain. What was it about Stasia? How could she do that? Bill had seen lots of babies before.

Soon after this, Brian's mom related another story that was similar. She is the kind of lady who makes a beehive look like Mexican siesta time. She goes grocery shopping every day just to have something to do. She is a whirl of movement wherever she goes. She talks and races about like a boy with a new firetruck. She just can't stand to sit still.

One day Mom called and told me, "You know I volunteer in the gift shop down at the hospital in Alexandria. And once a day, almost every time I'm in there, this little retarded girl comes in with a dollar to buy something. It always aggravates me because after giving her change, she stands there in line counting it for what seems like forever. And of course she's slow, and everyone knows it, but that doesn't make it any easier because everyone behind her sighs and looks very exasperated and disgusted, just wishing I'd get her out of there. I too get extremely impatient and try to rush her out.

"But after getting to know Stasia, something happened. I guess I just realized kindness and love and gentleness are a lot more important than rushing people through the checkout line. I don't know why I never thought that before. But when that little retarded girl came in, my attitude just became different. I began talking to her, helping her with the change, and if people in line didn't like it, too bad! She's a really nice girl, and I got to know her. She even calls me by name.

"Alsie, I tell you, I don't understand it . . . It's just that little Stasia makes a person realize how helpless she is, and we have to give such people room to be themselves. I don't understand it, but knowing her has changed me. I wanted you to know that, honey. That baby just sitting there on all those pillows is doing something to people."

She laughed and concluded, "That little Stasia . . . She's really something. And to think she never even had to preach a sermon about it. Just looking at her, you want to be different."

I smiled through my own tears as I realized my daughter was having an effect on other people that no one seemed quite able to explain. Although we often referred to her as "our little angel," we knew she was just one more of God's children reflecting the love, compassion, hope, and goodness that is in His own heart.

The End of Time
in our Home

WITNESSING THIS SUBTLE IMPACT that Stasia was having on others, I began to change in other ways. Those long hours dreaming and thinking and meditating in the rocker with Stasia asleep in my arms became a time to project myself into Stasia's world and imagine what the baby might be seeing and hearing and thinking. Often she became extremely tense and tight, swinging her head back and forth in agitation. This happened especially hearing loud noises or if she was picked up too quickly. I wanted to teach Stasia to relax and be at peace. But how?

As I thought about it, I realized that in a normal birth the child comes into the world out of a secure womb where everything had been provided automatically, every need met without so much as a whisper. Then suddenly the infant finds herself in this harshly bright place with these "things" moving about, strange noises resonating around her, and she doesn't know at all what it is. When a parent goes away, the infant has no idea of him or her "coming back" or being gone for "just a minute." All she knows is that her source of nurture and food and comfort is gone. It must be terrifying during those first few hours and days because she has no reference point to understand what's happening. All she knows is that it's either dark or light, the people are there or not there, the hunger pains are striking or not.

But eventually the child learns that at a cry Mom comes back. She learns to recognize voices and faces and such.

I compared this picture to Stasia. She couldn't learn. She couldn't process any of that. She only had 10 percent of her brain, just enough to react to the basic stimuli of life. How great would her terror be? Every day was new. She could not remember and make adjustments and compare this with that. Every moment was in some way different and perhaps, above all, terrifying.

In this respect one of Stasia's personal character traits was her inability to understand abrupt movement. If someone walked over to her and touched her, she'd flinch; she'd become terribly startled and even upset. I tried to figure this out, and eventually I learned to talk as I walked toward her: "It's me, Scooby-doo . . . Mommy. I'm going to pick you up now. See, that's my hand, and I'm going to touch your arm, so don't be afraid."

Still, who knew what she thought, how much she could remember, what connections she made to stimuli? Yes, in time she had begun giving individualized responses to Brian, me, and my mother. But in a sense Stasia was vastly different from us. Things must have come at her as a glob of color she couldn't pick apart or recognize. She couldn't identify them as people or children or dogs or whatever. They were strangers. Could she think of a place as a "room" and another place like it as "another room"? Or was it a whole new world, a whole new universe where she could never be sure what would be coming at her?

As I mulled over these insights, I decided that a whole new way of doing things was necessary. So I told Brian and my mother, "We don't know what she's thinking. We don't even know if she's thinking at all. We know she sees things. We know she likes music and that she can hear. But we're going to do something completely different in this house.

"From this moment forward, time has ceased to exist. Nothing is more important than this child's needs. We need to help her to trust and be at peace. The only way we can do that is to make time irrelevant."

My mother interrupted, but I held up my hand. "Let me finish, Mom, this is important. What I'm saying is that everything from now on is in slow motion. Don't touch Stasia until you've spoken to her. Then very gently touch her. When you help her put on a shirt, put your hand through the sleeve and slowly draw her hand back through. Everything will be done with complete gentleness and tender empathy around here. We have to help her trust us and not be afraid."

It was an interesting idea, and not one without difficulties, but we all decided to give it a try. After all, I had once thought about being a ballerina, and Brian wouldn't have minded being married to one!

The result was that Brian learned to talk to Stasia gently and clearly as he came into the room, announcing every turn and movement. "This is Daddy, Stasia. I'm walking over to you now. Now I'm getting close. Now I'm right over you—see? And here's my hand—whoo—feel it there on your arm. Yes, I can tell you do. Now I'm going to pick you up. Ready—one, two, three— wheeeee!"

The monologues could get comical at times too.

"Here we go. Coming in for a landing." He'd put her down gently and say, "Crrrrrr-aassssssssshhhhhhh."

By the second year Stasia knew what all these little monologues were about, and though she gave little indication of her feelings at the time, she seemed to be doing the thing we most wanted. That is, she wasn't afraid anymore; she *trusted*. She wasn't crying as much—in fact, quite rarely. That startled look, full of fear and anxiety, had disappeared.

Dr. Freeman had told Brian and me over and over that Stasia was incapable of thinking on any level. She did not have thoughts; she had reactions.

But this seemed to be proof to me that Stasia had to experience some kind of thought that told her, "This is like it was before; it's okay; there's no problem." What else could it be? She was learning. It wasn't just instinct. She was a little person.

Indeed, Stasia seemed to be learning to trust us both. She was no longer bound by the dark and the new and the strange. It was like another Scripture that I had learned recently: "Trust in the Lord with all your heart, and do not lean on your own understanding; in all your ways acknowledge Him, and He will make your paths straight."

The transformation all this gentleness and tenderness and slowness wrought on the home front didn't register until one day a friend, Don Speake, who was an elder at Chapelgate, commented on it. As he sat in the family room talking to Brian and watching me with the baby, he suddenly laughed with a characteristic rumble. As a big man and a famous tenor, at least in our church, his laugh was something to hear. He said, "Alsie, watching you is like watching ballet—poetry in motion. I've never seen anything like that with a baby. It's perfectly choreographed, like you've planned every step."

I only laughed and said, "I think I have."

The family had become a walking, living, and breathing choreography. Our motions were slow, methodical, always careful not to plop into Stasia's world like hurled stones and make her afraid again. It was just another of those adjustments one makes in creating a world of joy for another. It didn't even seem like a sacrifice, because we were beginning to function like a family again. Time had truly ceased in our home.

The Rose and
Other Little
Things

NOT LONG THEREAFTER, another interesting thing happened during a visit to the hospital. Taking a break one morning, I walked down to the Neurology Clinic to say hello to Georgia, the receptionist there, and anyone else at hand. We'd become good friends because of all the time we spent in the Clinic, so when Georgia learned of Stasia's latest illness, she immediately wanted to get her a gift, something to make the stay a little easier. She said to me, "How about a balloon?"

I shook my head. "No, Stasia can't really see it."

One of Stasia's special pleasures, though, came through her keen sense of smell. Often I would bring her a flower and set it under her nose, or dip cotton balls into vanilla or orange extract. Stasia's eyes would grow wide with pleasure and astonishment.

As I talked, Georgia said, "I'll get her a rose. Has she ever had a rose?"

"No, not that I can remember."

Georgia hurried down to the gift shop, found a rose, and stripped out all the prickers. When she came up to the hospital room, she started to hand the rose to me, but I said, "No, go ahead. You give it to her. Just go slow and tell her who you are before you touch her. She startles easily. Keep talking until you're close, then touch her arm."

Georgia moved forward slowly, spoke softly, and then gently touched Stasia's arm. She placed the rose right under her nostrils.

Instantly Stasia's eyes grew big, her eyebrows shot up, and the twitch of a smile was on her lips.

"Wow," Georgia commented. "How I'd like to get that kind of response out of someone, preferably male."

I laughed. This kind of response always amazed everyone around Stasia. She was so placid and peaceful most of the time, never responding to anything.

*

Dr. Freeman continued his assault on Brian and me about making time for fun and intimacy alone. I remained recalcitrant about the fact that I felt Stasia should always get the first and best and last of my day. Dr. Freeman called this classic obsessive-compulsive behavior, and in fact whenever he introduced us to new doctors or personnel in the clinic, he'd often say, "This is Alsie Kelley, as you know. She gives lessons in obsessive-compulsive behavior, so if you'd like to learn, she's the best in her field."

If that didn't get enough laughter, he'd add, "She might even let you touch her baby before she leaves. I've gotten to hold her twice in the last two years myself, so you'll realize it's quite a gift."

Dr. Freeman finally persuaded us to take a short jaunt away from home and Stasia and diapers and feeding machines and everything else. Thus one Valentine's Day when Stasia was coming up on her second birthday, we decided to take the plunge. Brian's parents offered to take Stasia for the night and the next day, if only I and Brian could get her and all her equipment down to their house in Alexandria, Virginia.

Brian filled our entire car with Stasia's gear—medications, emergency items, the feeding machine, bathing articles, everything she needed on a daily basis. We planned to go out to eat and stay overnight at a hotel in Washington, D.C. As always, I left them with every phone number I kept by the phone at home, as well as the number of the restaurant.

After demonstrating how everything worked, Brian and I set out with trepidation in our souls. We'd never tried this before. It would only be an experiment. But Dr. Freeman was right—we needed time together. We hadn't had a real date with one another in the two years since Stasia was born.

The first phone call came about two minutes after we arrived at the restaurant. The maitre d' found us and said Brian's mother was on the phone.

"It's the beeper on the feeding machine, Alsie," Mom explained. "It keeps going off. We think we're killing her."

Whenever formula clogged in the tube and didn't reach Stasia's stomach, the beeper would go off. I explained what the problem was. That settled, we took our seats and checked the menu which the maitre d' gave us. Three minutes later there was another call.

"Yes, Mrs. Kelley, same party," the maitre d' explained. He led me back to the phone.

"It started beeping again, honey. What are we doing wrong?"

Going through a list of possible reasons, I again solved it, returned to the table, and told Brian it was nothing to worry about—just the beeper.

Brian and I ordered, but there was the maitre d' back at the side of our table. "I'm very sorry, Mrs. Kelley, but you have another call."

He was obviously having a hard time keeping his composure, but Brian and I were beginning to find it quite amusing. And once again we found the solution to the persnickety beeper.

The meal was served. "Peace at last," Brian said.

I looked up. The maitre d' was once again walking toward our table. "Yes, Mrs. Kelley, same party. Can I do anything?"

The poor man was obviously rattled and very concerned, so I took the time upon my return to explain the situation and tell him about Stasia. He was sympathetic, and I repeatedly assured him all was well, there was nothing to worry about.

When we left, the maitre d' smiled at us and thanked us, saying, "It's not typical in my line of business, but tonight we've gotten to know one another quite well!"

Brian and I laughed. It was a good night, and something we needed. Although we decided not to spend the night at the hotel and returned to Brian's parents' house, once again Stasia or our guardian angel or someone who liked pranks had injected a little humor into our usually worry-riddled existence.

Florida

IN MARCH 1989 Brian learned his grandfather was dying in Florida. He was in his nineties and very frail. Brian had always been his grandfather's favorite, being the youngest and supposedly the cutest and most vulnerable of his grandchildren. He spent many summers as a child with Papa and Grandma Kelley in Boston. Frequently in his old age Papa would hug Brian and weep, then look at me and say, "Are you taking good care of him?"

I'd answer, "Of course, Papa," and that seemed to satisfy him.

When Stasia was born, Brian's Uncle Joe brought Papa to the hospital to see her in the NICU. The elderly man shook badly and sat in a wheelchair. He balked at holding our little girl, but everyone assured him it was okay. Finally we placed Stasia in his arms. He wept over the sight. Then when Uncle Joe wheeled him out, he reached up and gently grabbed a nurse on the arm. With tears in his eyes, he said to me, "Be sure to take care of that little girl— she's my great-granddaughter."

When we received news of Papa's condition, Brian told me, "We have to go. I have to see him." We thought about making plans to go down in April.

Both grandmothers agreed to watch Stasia for the few days Brian and I would be traveling, and we had a nurse for the midnight to 7 A.M. shift. It was the first time either of us would be away from Stasia for more than twenty-four hours, and I was on the verge of hysteria.

I knew we needed a break. And Brian's special relationship with Papa required that we go.

Brian called Larry McCloskey, who was the controller at the plush Hyatt Grand Cypress Hotel in Orlando, to see if he could get us a place in Miami where Papa lived. In the course of the conversation Larry also mentioned that if we ever wanted to come to Orlando, he could make the arrangements for a room at the Grand Cypress. Brian and I had both known Larry for several years because he and Brian had worked together in Baltimore. They had kept up their friendship over the years, and he knew quite a bit about our situation with Stasia.

Unfortunately, Papa died before we had a chance to fly out. The funeral took place in Boston at the end of March. It was a beautiful ceremony. However, during the service I began weeping almost uncontrollably. I missed Papa, of course, but more than that, I knew once again that someday, perhaps soon, I'd have to go through this with Stasia. Brian's Aunt Mary turned around in her seat and patted me on the knee, and that was comforting, but the picture stuck in my mind.

After the funeral, though, Brian told me, "Let's still go to Florida. I think we need to."

At the end of April, on a Thursday, we planned to fly down to Orlando in the morning. Brian's mother would arrive about 7 A.M., so we spent half the night packing, then fell into a dead sleep.

What seemed only seconds after turning the lights out, I suddenly awakened from a dream, having heard a strange sound. "What's that, Brian?"

He rolled out of bed and listened. "Someone's knocking at the door."

"Who could be knocking at this hour?" I was still too sleepy-eyed to focus on the bedside clock.

"I'll check."

A minute later he was back.

"Who is it?"

'My mother."

"Your mother!"

"We overslept. It's 7 A.M. We have less than forty-five minutes to get to the airport!"

We were both instantly awake, galvanized for action, and terrified we'd miss the flight. Somehow we threw everything together, got into the car with Brian's mother, and barreled out of the driveway bent on making that flight. When we reached the airport and checked in, we knew we were late. The check-in lady called ahead, telling the flight attendant we were on our way. We sprinted through the airport (literally like O. J. Simpson in that TV commercial!), and the moment we stepped onto the plane, the door closed and the plane taxied out onto the runway. How we ever got there in time is beyond me.

As soon as we disembarked in Orlando, I insisted that we call home to see how the baby was. I was still fearful of leaving the baby for a few days. Brian rolled his eyes with some exasperation, but he understood, so we found a phone booth. I called the grandmas, and Brian's mother answered. "Where are you?"

"In Orlando."

"No, you're not. No way you made that flight. Where are you really?"

"In Orlando, Mom. Is everything all right?"

"Everything's okay here, but where are you really?"

I insisted we were definitely in Orlando and we'd made the flight. To this day, Brian's mother is convinced we couldn't have made the flight and assures us she's going to find out one day where we really were. But we were on our way to our first real vacation in several years.

Neither of us had ever been to the Hyatt Grand Cypress before, but upon stepping into the huge foyer of the hotel, we felt as if we'd both catapulted into another world. Inside the hotel were half a dozen very expensive, gourmet specialty restaurants, each one a five-star rated marvel. There were three pools, by my count. The hotel also featured its own private golf course. (This is not a commercial for the Grand Cypress; however, it was truly an incredible sight to me.) DisneyWorld was down the road, and undoubtedly shuttles were provided, though we never made it to that particular site during our time there.

As soon as we checked in, Larry met us at the front desk and gave us a tour of the entire hotel. We made plans to have dinner with him that night at one of the restaurants. He concluded the tour by taking us to our room, which was a two-room suite. The suite was laid out with two bathrooms, a bedroom with a king-sized bed, a sitting room, monstrous closets, a kitchenette, and a wet bar. A balcony enclosed the three sides of the room as they gazed out upon one of the lavish pools to our eyes' and hearts' delight. Each day we found a dozen new roses in vases in each bathroom, and, at the foot of the bed, another bouquet of roses. Before bedtime another attendant laid one salmon-colored rose on each pillow. At the same time they left a glass tray at the foot of the bed laden with a display of French pastries in the shapes of animals. Every night they also left an expensive bottle of liqueur, soda pop on ice, and Perrier. There was a refrigerator filled with all kinds of drinks.

I wanted to call home nearly every hour to see how Stasia was, but Brian insisted on the two-call limit, and I grudgingly complied. In one of the calls, I mentioned the room and the amenities and the liqueurs. Brian's mother laughed and said, "What a terrible thing to waste expensive liqueur on someone who doesn't drink!"

Shortly after we arrived, a giant fruit basket was delivered. This particular piece of hotel beneficence consisted of Toblerones, chocolates, strawberries, apples, grapefruit, oranges, raspberries— every one larger than life, the kind of fruit that wins prizes each year at State Fairs. Over the course of the next few days, I'd take one bite, set the piece down, and forget about it for a while. We'd come back from a jaunt, and the partially eaten fruit would be gone—replaced by another sumptuous layout. We were, to say the least, walking around in a state of complete astonishment.

There were paddleboats out on the lakes with swans lazily floating about. The designers of the hotel had also imported a turn-of-the-century trolley from Brussels and reconstructed it on site. The whole setup seemed grandiose and unthinkably expensive.

We both tried to put the money question out of our minds. After all, we hadn't had a vacation in years. We spent most of our time at the hotel, luxuriating in fabulous meals and intimate conversations about everything we'd missed discussing for the last two years. It seemed as if our marriage was renewed in ways we couldn't have anticipated. Our closeness deepened, and I found myself for the moment falling in love all over again.

On Sunday the hotel offered a champagne brunch with formal attire, costing over fifty dollars per person. The whole time there Brian signed the bills to be charged to our room, but in a way both of us felt as if we were signing away our lives. We kept telling one another we needed this, though, and determined not to let the money issue intrude.

Then came Monday morning, our last hour there. At breakfast I wept. For the first time in years I remembered what it had been like when it was just Brian and me, in love, carefree, intimate, best friends. I loved Stasia more than my own life. I missed her terribly and wanted to go back. It had been agony to only call twice a day. But what Brian and I had felt for one another, what we'd seen again in our marriage—the lone spark had become a bonfire again, and I didn't want to lose it. For so long I'd felt and believed our marriage was over.

Somehow we muddled through breakfast and packed, Brian giving me verbal encouragement all the way. Then we returned to the lobby to pay the bill. Both of us were sinking lower and lower. I was sure we were bankrupt.

Brian stepped white-faced to the desk while I stood with the luggage, my arms hugging my shoulders like a homeless child in despair. Brian stood there and pulled out his wallet. As I watched, there were some long exchanges, and I prayed, "Please don't let us be bankrupt, Lord."

A moment later Brian turned and walked back toward me, his face even whiter. I said, "How bad is it?"

Brian answered, "It's been taken care of."

Shaking my head adamantly, I said, "No, you can tell me, Brian, don't spare me—how much was it?"

"It's been taken care of, I said."

"Please, Brian, don't mess with this. I'm your wife. You can tell me."

Brian suddenly cracked a grin after the fifth go-round. "Alsie, Larry took care of it. The entire bill."

I dropped my jaw. "Brian, he'll get fired."

Brian just shook his head. "He wanted to do it."

As a child, Larry had a brother who was mentally retarded. When he was born in the 1950s, the doctors told Larry's mother to put the boy in an institution. That was the way back then. She wouldn't do it. Larry's parents chose to raise Larry, his sister, and his handicapped brother all by themselves, which became even more difficult for his mother when his father died at a young age. Larry later told Brian, "I know what it's like in your situation. I know about the money, about never having time for anything, for yourself, or anyone else. And about the worry, the pain, the constant problems. It's my treat."

The Insurance Companies

BACK IN COLUMBIA, Stasia began to grow steadily and to gain weight because of the gastrostomy. She turned two in May and continued growing, up past twenty pounds. Again I assured myself we were finally winning the battle. Somehow Stasia would lead a relatively normal life. I was convinced there was a way and that God would lead us to it. Dr. Freeman had to be wrong; Stasia had the same chance at life as any other handicapped child. I was being completely unrealistic, but I sensed that even Dr. Freeman admired my tenacity.

At the same time, though, I didn't realize that my own clutch on Stasia had tightened. That first year I had prayed, "God, please keep Stasia through the night. And if You take her, take her gently and swiftly."

Lately, however, I'd become aware of a slight tightening in my grip on her little life. I still prayed that God would see her safely through the night—but that was all. She was mine, and He could not have her.

There were other pressing problems, though, besides Stasia's immediate health. Brian and I were still worn-out, despite the welcomed respite in Orlando. One of the biggest problems was our insurance. We had been completely unable to convince our medical insurance company that a day nurse was warranted and needed. We were continually turned down. Through spates of argument and pressure and all manner of persuasion that I could muster, I repeatedly told the adjusters, "We're running an ICU here. This child is severely handicapped. We need someone qualified to help in the home."

Our insurance company would only approve coverage, though, if Stasia was hospitalized or institutionalized. This is a typical problem for people in our situation (though I didn't know that at the time), with few getting the kind of results and help they need. If we didn't get turned down outright, we were the brunt of an endless paperwork runaround that left us frustrated and angry. On top of that, the company bureaucracy made it only more exasperating. There was constant arguing and threatening, promises of action and then no tangible results. The biggest issue was, "usual and customary," a legal phrase anyone who has battled a medical insurance company quickly becomes familiar with. Claim forms would come back with a multitude of uncovered charges. And why? Because they were beyond "the usual and customary" charges for such procedures. Furthermore, many procedures and expenses such as in-house nursing were not "usual and customary" and therefore not covered. I determined to find a way to break the code.

By what seemed chance—which I increasingly interpreted as the sovereignty and providence of God—I learned one day on a trip to Baltimore that Columbia, now our home community, was also the base of the Cedar Lane School, a well-known and respected facility for teaching children with handicaps. I called Cedar Lane right away, and they sent out a teacher to evaluate Stasia. Because Stasia's immune system was so poorly developed and she was so susceptible to illnesses, we knew she would never go to that school, or in all probability to any school.

Cedar Lane gave us a brochure about the state-sponsored Maryland Infant and Toddlers Program for the Handicapped.

Prior to this, I had been shuffled from government agency to agency with no concrete help whatsoever. The teacher explained that the Cedar Lane program was only in the pilot stages, and it was full. But they were looking for multiple-handicapped children.

I lit up. Who, if not Stasia, could qualify for that?

A second problem, the teacher explained, was that Stasia was almost two years old now, and their program stopped at age two. I told her, "My child won't even live for another year. She only has 10 percent of her brain. The only organs in her body that work well are her lungs and heart."

The teacher was sympathetic, and she sent us to an all-day seminar in Calverton, Maryland, sponsored by the state program. One of the courses listed was, "How to Get Cooperation from Your Insurance Company."

This was an incredible gift to Brian and me, for it taught us how to deal with the "usual and customary" clauses in contracts that companies always nail you with—the very problem we were having.

It was through this seminar that I learned about a single woman who was a nurse and had adopted three handicapped children. Her name was Jude Linthicum. On our first contact by phone, Jude told me, "With many insurance companies you're reduced to playing chicken. When you go into the hospital, you find that they'll release you early just to get out of the high bills. So what do you do? You request help in the home. And then the insurance company says, 'Not usual and customary for this condition.' So you play chicken. You say, 'Okay, you will only pay when she's in the hospital, so we'll keep her in the hospital until you recognize it's better to pay the cost of in-home care than in-hospital care.' That's basically what you've got to do. There's a price. You may have your child in the hospital a long time. They may wait you out. But they might be paying thousands of dollars a day for that, when they could be getting away with a couple hundred dollars for in-home nursing care. It's nuts, but that's the way it is."

I stomped around the house shouting, "Hallelujah" on the one hand and declaring all-out war on the other. The other big problem, though, was that Brian's employer frequently changed insurance companies. Nearly every year because of skyrocketing costs of medical coverage, employers like Brian's found they could not get medical insurance on a cost-effective basis. No insurance company would take on a corporation with people like us on their list for long without increasing their rates or canceling altogether. This was another problem I knew would eventually come up. But Jude had help in that area too.

Jude and I talked frequently after that. All three of Jude's children were handicapped, and she had gotten full-time in-home care!

"How did you do it?" I asked incredulously.

"Well, what have you done?"

I answered, "I had the doctor write a letter."

"Right, and how long was it?"

"About three lines."

Jude laughed. "That's about as far as they'll go on their own. Doctors will hardly write their own signatures happily and legibly, let alone ten lines out of their own brains. So this is what you do. Sit down and write out a letter and give a detailed outline of every major bodily system in Stasia that has problems. Then you need to show what kind of nursing care is required for the maintenance of each system. Then outline how many hours a day it will take to do this. Do your research. Then . . ."

I was almost breathless. How did Jude know this? "Then?"

"Then get your doctor to sign it."

"He will?"

"Of course. If it's the truth, and if he knows your child, he'll be glad to."

Jude came out to the house and helped me write that letter. It was four typed pages, a veritable dissertation on Stasia Kelley. I took it to Dr. Scott Strahlmann, our pediatrician at the Columbia

Medical Plan. I asked him if he'd look it over and consider signing it. After reading it, Dr. Strahlmann said, "I'd be delighted."

I sent it in.

The insurance company lost it several times. I called Hartford, Atlanta, the office in Baltimore, everywhere. Finally they found it and said, "We're not in the baby-sitting business!"

I argued, talked to different adjusters, and went through the letter line by line with them—when it was finally found—four more times. Finally they approved a nurse and twenty-four-hour care. But they asked, "How soon will the nursing end?"

In my frustration I answered, "It's not going to end. This is it, unless a miracle happens!"

That threw another glitch into the machinery.

"What do you mean it's not going to end? We have to put a cap on this."

"Sorry," I said. "She's not getting better."

This really jammed up the works. The insurance company stalled and stalled and stalled. The frustration mounted. I went to Jude and learned about another tactic. "Tell them to send an insurance adjuster right to your home for twenty-four hours."

The adjuster never came. However, twenty-four hours later we had a letter which said they'd provide nursing care in the home for as long as it was necessary. But it had to go through one last barrier: board approval.

We waited for several days, and then I called. They'd lost the letter! I called the Atlanta office, then the Connecticut office; it went back and forth. After hours of confrontation, aggressiveness, and downright nastiness, they found it and told me, "The board has to meet. It'll be settled within thirty days."

Thirty more days! It was impossible. And ridiculous. And wrong!

Brian and I went back to Jude. "What can we do now?"

She answered, "The next time Stasia is admitted to the hospital, talk to the doctor. If he thinks it's warranted he'll order the in-home nursing hours and keep her until the insurance company relents."

I shook my head with despair. "Jude, this is the longest period in Stasia's life that she's been out of a major hospital, just four months. How long could this last? Do you know what it does to us to see her in a place like that? I know it's a great hospital, but Stasia won't get the kind of love and attention she's used to and that we can give if we just had some help."

Jude had no more suggestions.

It was then that I got mad, about as mad as I can get, which by now you understand is quite mad. I stalked into the house that afternoon and dialed the number of the insurance company's main office. When someone answered, I asked to talk to the manager, and then I unloaded. "Okay, here's how it is—I sent you three copies of this letter, not the original, and you lost all three copies. I'm sending you one more set of three copies. You have ten days. If I don't hear from you, I'm going to call the local news stations— Channel 11, Channel 2, and Channel 13 here in Baltimore. They love this kind of thing. I'm sure you've seen how they've decapitated a few companies like yours when they broadcast names, dates and places of rank injustice."

I didn't give the man a second to catch his breath.

"After I get them onto the story, I'll go to the nationals—NBC, CBS, ABC, and I'll even try CNN. I hear they like this kind of thing, too. After that I'll call the governor of Maryland—you know, Donald Schaeffer, the guy who as mayor of Baltimore used to drive around looking for potholes. Oh, he's a doozy, I'll tell you. But in my case, you see, he's a friend of our family. So it's like a little favor here. But of course, I'll let our U.S. Congressman and Senators know, too. They're also friends of the family. You realize this is a political year, and politicians love to dig their claws into stuff like this."

The man tried to break in several times, but I repeatedly told him, "Wait, I'm not finished yet—there are several more things you should know. You see, I don't work outside the home. And I have lots and lots of time to call all these people. In fact, I almost have nothing else to do at the moment. So you see, this might even turn out to be a little fun."

Within twenty-four hours we had a *carte blanche* contract for full-time nursing care.

Now the problem was, where to look. After what seemed like an endless series of less than satisfactory interviews I finally stumbled upon God's choice for the position. Enter Liloutie Price.

Lil

LIL HAD BEEN THE DIRECTOR of a nursing home. She had burned out on that job after several years and was now working for an agency. She wanted to get back on the personal side of nursing care, not the administrative side. One of the women I had interviewed earlier told Lil about the job. "Why don't you take it, Lil? It sounds perfect for you."

When Lil came that Saturday for the interview, I am convinced that if I'd opened the door five minutes ahead of her knock, I would have seen God forming her out of the dust. She was the most gentle, compassionate person I've ever known, and she gained those qualities through suffering. She was perfect for what we needed, and for what *I* needed.

People would often say of Lil, "There's such an air of peace about her."

We hired her right away, and she started on the following Monday. Dark-skinned, in her forties, she had two boys and a little girl. She'd also lost a son through leukemia, and her husband James had died several years later. She is soft-spoken with very dark eyes and black hair tinged with gray. Often she and I would talk about spiritual and personal matters that I had never discussed with any other woman in my life.

One day I asked her about this air of peace she had, and she said,

"It comes from reliance on the Lord. It happens when He strips you of everything. I had to watch my ten-year-old son die of leukemia over a period of eleven months. Three years later my husband died of a heart attack. I was left with three children, ages two, six, and eight. What do you do then? You lean on God or you die."

On other occasions Lil would tell me, "I'm a very stubborn person . . . like you."

I never believed it. "You are the most peaceful, placid person I've ever met. What do you mean?"

In her Trinidadian accent Lil would always reply, "When God breaks you, it happens."

Thus I began the difficult business of transferring authority to this tiny dark woman with a great heart and spirit. Brian especially was nervous about the situation, knowing well how protective I could be. He was concerned that Lil's nursing skills would be undermined by me hovering about watching every move. However, he decided to give it a few days.

Then on Wednesday afternoon he called. "So how's Lil working out, Alsie?"

"I'm not sure," I answered with surprising vagueness.

"Well, do you think there's a problem?"

"She's not doing anything, Brian. I'm doing everything. She sits down there reading magazines all afternoon."

Taking a deep breath, Brian plodded along. "Let me ask you a question—are you letting her do anything?"

"I don't want her to touch the baby!"

Brian laughed. "A nurse has to touch the baby. Good grief, Alsie! Why are you surprised she's reading magazines if you're not letting her do anything?"

"I can't turn Stasia over to just anybody, Brian."

"So show her how you want her to do it, and then let her do it." Brian obviously felt both amused and exasperated by my inflexibility and downright unreasonableness. I finally began showing Lil

Stasia's and my fine-tuned choreography, and she took it up with zest and commitment.

In a few days Lil was competently and gently going about doing all the things I needed her for, using the same ballet movements I had already perfected. After a week or so of struggle to find out who each other was, Lil and I learned to talk on a level I had never experienced with another woman. The possibility of Stasia's death was always on my mind, and Lil, having lost a son and a husband in three years, was a perfect sounding board for my fearful questions.

One day I asked her, "Lil, what do you do when a child dies?"

Lil thought for a while and finally answered succinctly, "You hurt, and then you lean on God, and then you heal."

After thinking about the meaning in that statement, I asked tentatively, "Which was worse, losing your husband or your son?"

Again Lil thought, but her answer this time was not as short. "Both are painful. Both are breaking. It hurt for a long time, but God worked, and I healed, and I go on."

I found her answer astonishing, but her obvious faith drew me close, and I trusted her judgment and her advice.

On another occasion I said, "If you had anything to change while James was still alive, what would it be?"

Again Lil thought as though studying her answer out in her mind before actually sending it to her lips. Finally she answered, "I would have changed the distance. For three years we each went in our own separate directions to heal from the loss of our son. That was not good. We lost our sense of each other. I would have compressed it into Fast Forward, held him more, loved him more. If only we had gone the road together, it would not have taken as long. So the distance I would have changed, yes."

Lil was Stasia's nurse, my closest friend, counselor, teacher, mother confessor, spiritual advisor, provider of hope, bringer of peace . . . Ah yes, that was one of her more interesting roles and a rather interesting phenomenon. Lil was in our home five days a week, Monday through Friday from 8:30 A.M. to 4:30 P.M. All day long while she was there with me and helping to take care of Stasia she'd be silently interceding in prayer for us with the Father. When Brian and I left the house she'd go through every room and pray. Our weeks usually passed relatively peacefully. But on Friday evening and all through the weekend it was as if all Hell had broken loose and chaos reigned, bitter angry arguments ensued, and tempers were short. Then on Monday, Lil would hear all about the weekend and she'd start praying. Peace would come into our home once again. It got so I didn't want to let her go home on Fridays. I'd think up things for her to help me with, pleading my inability to do them alone.

And then there was her role as marital counselor. Bless her for that one. If not for Lil, I am absolutely conviced Brian and I would not be together today. Lil was family and soon enough picked up on the tension between Brian and me. She got to know us at the lowest point of our marriage. Brian was sleeping down the hall in the guest room, we were barely talking, and when we did it was in bitter and caustic tones. Lil, more than anyone, understood what losing a child can do to a marriage. She knew we needed time alone together, but there was no one I felt comfortable leaving Stasia with—no one of course except Lil. Stasia's care was becoming more complicated as she deteriorated. Although she was gaining weight, she was still a newborn with no body control or head control whatsoever. I had noticed a subtle change in Lil's attitude and manner toward Stasia over the weeks and months that she'd been with us. She was becoming increasingly attached and very protective toward Stasia. It got to be a game with us to see who could get to her first when she woke up. Of equal significance to me was Lil's nursing skill and personal experience. I felt secure in the knowledge that Lil would know what to do if an emergency arose or worse . . . Having been through it, I knew she'd know what to do.

Labor Day weekend that year was particularly bad. I had given

Lil the whole weekend off. But that Friday I was extremely depressed, and Lil had seen it. It seemed that I was depressed a lot.

So Lil showed up on Labor Day Monday. "I've sent the kids to camp," she explained. "You two need some time together."

Both Brian and I tried to talk her out of it. "You need time alone, too, Lil. You should get a few days off now and then."

But Lil would explain, "Here I feel peace. Here is Stasia, a little angel, and peace. I need that too. Go . . . Please."

She cared for Stasia the whole day, while Brian and I went to a mall and walked around, then took in a movie that night. We had a delightful evening, once again only tasting some of the bliss we'd felt as a family but which always seemed to go when the pressures at home interfered. It was a magnificent, personal gift only Lil could give.

Bronchitis

LIL AND I HAD COME TO VIEW our time together as a mutual time of healing. Lil's favortie time of the day in our household was when she was sitting at the kitchen table writing medical notes about Stasia and gazing out the picture window at the trees below. "It's such a place of peace," she often said. "My three kids," Lil would explain, "I love them, but I come here for the peace." She'd read her Bible, *Our Daily Bread*, or other devotionals while Stasia slept and stare out the window with a happy smile etched on her lips.

In the fall of 1989 Stasia began suffering from renewed intestinal problems and a sinus infection. I feared an impending hospital stay. Always the question lurking in the back of our minds whenever Stasia was admitted to the hospital was, *Would this be her last stay? Would she leave the hospital this time?* Stasia's second year of life had been wonderful. She'd been out of the hospital for almost a year, she was gaining weight, there had been no major difficulties, and the future looked promising. However, during the course of the fall, Stasia was beginning to show the telltale signs of illness—losing weight, looking pale and washed out, and sleeping more and more.

One day as I was helping Lil sterilize some of Stasia's things, I turned to her and said, "You know, Lil, I've come to the conclusion that I'll never be able to let Stasia go unless she's suffering horribly in the hospital."

Lil replied, "Alsie, don't say that! You have no idea how bad that can be. I do. I've been there. I wouldn't release my son to God's care, and before he died his skin was like tissue paper, and he was in constant pain. Don't be as foolish as I was."

"I can't help it, Lil. My grip on her has tightened so much, I don't think I could survive without her. I'll never let her go."

Lil never tried to coerce me into accepting any of her ideas, but this was one thing she knew I would have to deal with. My clutch on Stasia was strong, but that would not prevent the Lord from taking her when it was His will to do so. Lil bided her time and prayed.

I left the kitchen and went upstairs to get Stasia's bath things. As I descended the stairs a voice—audible or inaudible, I never knew—it was something like my vision of nearly a year before—spoke directly to me. The voice said, "From your arms to My arms."

No one was in the house but Lil and Stasia, and I knew it wasn't Lil's voice. For a moment I was paralyzed with terror, wondering first if I was "losing it," and second, if God was really saying something important to me. I wasn't sure what it meant, but I rushed in a panic into the kitchen and told Lil, with rising dread, "I think Stasia may be a lot sicker than we think."

Her illness continued to worsen over the next few months, and nothing either we or the doctors could do could halt the merciless onslaught. Finally over the weekend of February 3 and 4, 1990, her temperature skyrocketed to 104°. We fought desperately to bring it down but couldn't. We finally took her in to see Dr. Strahlman. After some anxious moments, Dr. Strahlman told us Stasia had bronchitis. We knew Stasia's condition could easily worsen. I remembered Dr. Freeman's fateful words of how death would probably come: "pneumonia." This was especially portentous because the combination of Stasia's weak immune system, limited lung capacity, and susceptibility to infections left her particularly defenseless. What was even worse was the fact that if blood had to be given or taken, her small veins made it almost impossible to get a solid IV hookup. That was always agony. When it came to Stasia, pneumonia was the illness we feared more than any other.

Over the next nine days a monumental struggle to keep the infection at bay ensued. I'd sit up at nights in the rocking chair by her crib listening to her labored breathing and feeling absolutely helpless. In the hours before dawn I would desperately try to think of something of great enough worth to offer God in exchange for my daughter's life. I would gladly have given my own life for Stasia's, but I'd already made that offer to God, to no avail.

One night I remembered a story Dr. Adams, our pastor, told me. He said that every night before he'd drift off to sleep he'd discuss his day with the Lord. One night as he was in the middle of going over some complicated church issues with the Lord, the Lord suddenly said, "Lane, you know I love you, and I'm truly interested in all that concerns you. But would you mind much if we continued this discussion tomorrow? I have had such a day with that Alsie Kelley!"

There was little else I could do during those long hours of the night but pray. I couldn't even hold Stasia in my arms because whenever we picked her up she'd begin to choke and gag. Every mother knows it is her sacred right, her highest responsibility, and her greatest joy to hold and comfort her baby. Was there nothing God would leave untouched? Was He determined to strip me of *everything*?

Saturday, February 10, 1990 was a cold, wet, dreary day both outside the nursery window and inside my aching heart. I began to plead with God for the billionth time to spare our baby's precious life. The room was warm and steamy from the vaporizer, and I dozed off. I awoke suddenly when I heard that same still, small voice I'd heard on the stairs a few weeks earlier, whether audible or inaudible I still don't know. There were only two words this time, just two words—"Bronchial pneumonia." I quickly looked around to see who was speaking, but Stasia and I were alone. As I turned to look out the window, in my mind's eye I saw a towering tidal wave coming toward the house at breakneck speed. I knew instantly what it all meant—the thing we'd feared most, pneumonia, was coming. I shuddered. If Stasia died, I knew somehow I'd be destroyed as well.

Brian and I called Dr. Strahlman, and he asked us if we wanted to admit Stasia to the hospital, but we decided against it because of the skeletal crew there on weekends.

However, a few days later, February 15, 1990, Brian and I once again rushed Stasia in to see Dr. Strahlman when we detected blood in her diaper. He examined Stasia while Brian stood in one corner of the waiting room and I in the other. Lil was sitting down in between us. For over two years now both Brian and I had dreaded this day, and suddenly we were retreating to our separate worlds again.

Then Dr. Strahlmann turned to speak to us, his face urgent. Looking back and forth from Brian to me, he finally gave us the terrible news: "I'm sorry. We've done our best, but it's pneumonia."

I looked across at Brian, his face ashen. Brian stared back at me. I was white with fright. Neither of us could move.

When Lil saw what was happening, she stood up. She walked behind Brian and pushed him toward me. Then she grabbed me and pulled us together. "Hold each other," she said. "This is a time to hold each other."

Both of us cried, with Lil's arms around us.

Dr. Strahlmann said, "We'll call Hopkins."

Hopkins didn't have a bed available. Within a few minutes the decision was made to take Stasia home, give her the necessary antibiotics and shots with Lil assisting; we would keep her on oxygen in our home ICU.

It was all set up, and during the night I kept a constant watch, listening to Stasia's lungs and heart with a stethoscope every hour.

Despite my efforts, the next morning Stasia was bleeding around her stomach tube.

I called Dr. Strahlmann again. He told us to get to Hopkins immediately. He would have his secretary call the ambulance.

Months before I had learned that in such an emergency we should not call 911. Law required ambulances from the emergency number to rush the patient to the nearest hospital, which in our community was Howard County General Hospital. But HCGH had no facilities or expertise in dealing with a child like Stasia, at least not on a regular basis; and besides, all our records were at Hopkins. I was always advised to call a private ambulance. They would take Stasia to whichever hospital we requested. I assumed that was what Dr. Strahlmann's secretary had done, because he was the one who originally informed us of the plan.

I called Brian and asked him to meet us at the Johns Hopkins emergency room.

As Lil and I gathered all the articles we needed and dressed the baby, I heard the siren outside. A female nurse and two men came to the door. The moment I saw the big golden letters and the numbers on the side of the ambulance, I knew it was not a private ambulance.

Forcing back the anger and fear, I led them upstairs. The nurse tried to get Stasia's blood pressure. There was none. She said, "Let's get going. We're on our way to Howard County."

"No," I said, "we're going to Hopkins."

The woman glanced at the two men. "No, ma'am, we're going to Howard County."

I explained, "They're all standing by at Hopkins. Dr. Freeman is waiting for us. We're going to Hopkins."

At that moment I noticed a "shift" in the look of all three of the emergency personnel in the room—a look I'd seen whenever I was working with medical people who thought they were dealing with a "hysterical woman." I didn't even wait for them to speak. "I know exactly what you're thinking. 'This is a hysterical woman. She doesn't know what she's saying. Humor her.' Look, I know you're from 911. I know legally you're supposed to go to Howard County. But they'll kill her there. We're going to Hopkins. I'm not hysterical."

The man stepped forward and touched me on the shoulder. "Ma'am, we know you're distraught. We . . ."

I moved away. "Don't you 'distraught' me! Howard County is not equipped to care for this child, and I don't have the time to convince you. She's in shock, and you can't get a blood pressure reading. We have to go to Hopkins. If you can't do it, then give me the papers—I'll sign them all and let you go. You're released. I'll drive to Hopkins myself."

"But, ma'am, we have to . . ."

"I can get to Hopkins in seventeen minutes. How soon can you get there?"

"That's all the way into Baltimore, ma'am. It's impossible." It was actually over eighteen miles away in the center of the city, with no main highways nearby.

"I've done it before," I insisted, "and I'll do it again."

Lil cringed in a corner, having already experienced one of my seventeen-minute rides. No rules were obeyed except getting there in one piece. She was praying desperately that God would intervene.

The paramedic said, "Let me get on the phone and get authorization."

I answered, "You have sixty seconds to get it or else we're out of here."

The man went to the phone, looking over his shoulder with exasperation and making eyes at his partners. I told myself not to think about it, and Lil began packing up our van. Then I picked up Stasia and was on the way out the nursery door when the man rushed back in. "We have authorization, ma'am. All the way into Hopkins. Let's go."

We flew down Route 95 into Baltimore. But as Lil and I sat

with the baby in the back, I listened to the men talking in the front. They didn't know how to get to Hopkins! They didn't even know what entrance to go to!

I pushed my way to the front of the ambulance. "Listen to me— I'll tell you how to get there." With me sitting on the hump between the two men, I directed them street by street to the children's emergency entrance. Lil was dizzy by the time we arrived at the emergency entrance.

There Dr. Freeman and Brian stood, waiting patiently for us. When the 911 ambulance pulled up, though, Dr. Freeman's mouth dropped open.

We rushed Stasia inside. For several hours the doctors worked feverishly over her to start an IV and stabilize her blood pressure and pulse. Once stabilized, she was moved out of the emergency room to another treatment room. Brian went home to get some clothing for staying overnight. I stayed with Stasia. A group of doctors came by every hour or so to watch the proceedings.

During that period Pastor Ron Steel, the new senior pastor at Chapelgate, arrived and sat out in the waiting room, watching and listening with our elder, Ian Chisholm.

Dr. Freeman was amazed I'd gotten the 911 ambulance to come to Hopkins. I smiled. "Dr. Freeman, have you ever known me not to get what I want where this child is concerned?"

He grinned and nodded with understanding. He said, "I have never seen a 911 come to Baltimore from Howard County before!"

But it was only a brief moment of respite. Stasia was stable but critically ill.

The Hospital

THE HOSPITAL ADMITTED STASIA, and we settled into the room, Brian planning to spend the night, while I would go home and return in the morning. By the next night Stasia was bleeding from every orifice. Her stomach had also shut down, so she could not take any food.

Everyone worked desperately to stop the bleeding. One IV vein had collapsed. Several others were rendered unusable. The only one left was borderline. As a result, the phenobarbital, which controlled Stasia's seizures, could not be administered. Stasia began seizing every few minutes, and it was impossible to stop the hemorrhaging. I well knew how much Stasia needed phenobarbital. Only through massive doses were the seizures ever controlled, even though at the same time no one knew what kind of effect it was having on Stasia's nervous system. It was a trade-off—a life with reasonable comfort and few of the jarring, nerve-wracking, body-binding seizures, or just the reverse, a horror of an existence with few possible benefits except that Stasia might have a greater awareness of her world. No one could be sure of that, though.

The truth was, the massive doses were critical. However, a new female doctor neither Brian or I knew was on that shift. She didn't understand about the dosage, Stasia's history, or the monumental decision-making process that had gone into determining the need for the drug. She demanded that they follow normal procedures.

"You're saying Stasia was administered a dose far above the normal level, Mrs. Kelley," she said. "That is patently wrong."

I knew it was fruitless to argue. "Please get Dr. Freeman on the phone."

"I can't do that."

"I have his phone number," I answered. "Do you want to call him or shall I?"

Normally no one had Dr. Freeman's personal number. In an emergency, maybe, just maybe someone on the unit would get the secret number and call, but that was rare. He already worked long hours as it was, and only the direst emergencies would require a personal call to his home.

However, Dr. Freeman had long ago given us his home phone number. Perhaps it was part of his understanding of Stasia's condition and the delicate nature of all the neurological episodes involving her. More than that, it was just something he understood about me. He wanted to be informed and involved in everything concerning Stasia's medical condition. That was the bottom line.

Swallowing apprehensively, the new doctor agreed to call Dr. Freeman herself. After explaining the situation, Dr. Freeman said, "Do it."

The doctor came back into the room, still a bit stunned. "Okay, we'll give her the dose."

She started to administer it through the IV. Moments later Stasia's vein collapsed. A nurse, a doctor, and Brian and I stood staring. There was only one place left to try, in the middle of Stasia's scalp. All the other veins were useless from repeated injections or the same kind of collapse. Stasia was seizing every few seconds now. Her whole body would clench, her face wrenching as if it might burst. The blood sprayed from the artery on her left wrist and innumerable other orifices. Her stomach was still shut down. She couldn't digest anything.

I couldn't believe we'd come this far just to have it all end here. Somehow in the midst of it all I got out a message to Pastor Ron Steel at Chapelgate. "Please get everyone praying," I said, then explained the situation.

The doctor worked on that single last vein in Stasia's scalp. Even as my little girl seized, the doctor patiently searched through the golden hair. As we watched, several people breathed in and out in unison.

When the doctor finally slid in the needle, I asked, "Is it in?"

"Yes."

"Will it hold?"

"We'll see."

Everyone waited, still breathless and silent. The vein didn't collapse. A few minutes later the seizures stopped. After a momentary round of silent cheering, the doctor said, "Now we've got to address this bleeding problem." She then told us the goal now was to make Stasia comfortable. We knew she meant death was very close.

The doctor turned around and went out to get some gauze, then came back. Everyone in the room was staring at the little form on the hospital bed. The bleeding had stopped. Just stopped.

No one breathed. The doctor touched the baby, but the blood flow had really ended. "Isn't that weird?" she said. "I've never seen anything like it."

As we all relaxed with new enthusiasm and hope, Brian stood in a corner watching and thinking. He knew in his heart this was only a brief respite. It might be miraculous, perhaps it was related to the phenobarbital, maybe even to the prayers of the people at the church. Who really knew? But he was sure it wouldn't last. He thought for the thousandth time how it would be when Stasia finally left us. He had an image in his mind of his daughter on a hospital operating table surrounded by nurses and doctors, performing CPR, while he and I were stuck away in a corner, ignored

. . . And little Stasia lying there without a single familiar face above or around her.

Over the last three years Brian and I had witnessed a number of deaths in that hospital, or at least the effects. That night in the PICU a year and a half before, when that grandfather staggered into the hallway and the wails of the mother broke the silence, had painted a picture in his mind of something he didn't want: hysterical parents . . . a pulverized little body . . . hopelessness and brokenness . . . a bloody, unwelcome death under glaring lights. The imagined scene tore him up.

Before Stasia's birth, Brian had prayed now and then as he and I went to church regularly. But as the problems, difficulties, and setbacks ransacked our lives after Stasia's birth, he'd come to believe that his prayers were all going unanswered. God didn't really answer prayer, so why pray? Everything good that did happen could be explained by luck, happenstance, coincidence. The last two years had convinced him that faith rarely worked, or at least it didn't work for him. The current crisis was just one more example of how futile his faith was.

Deep down, though, Brian wanted to believe that God was there, that, as I believed, there was purpose in all this agony, and that God did indeed answer prayer. He couldn't shake that hope, even though it mostly drowned in his accountant's listing of all the failures and horrors of life he'd seen.

Suddenly as Brian stood in the corner of that hospital room, he knew what he longed for concerning our last moments together with our little angel. He didn't want her to die hooked up to a series of machines. He didn't want to prolong certain agony with devices. He knew there was nothing anyone could do to give Stasia a better or longer life. We'd already signed the forms that released the hospital from taking "extraordinary measures"—a DNR, "Do Not Resuscitate."

And so he prayed a brief but specific prayer in his mind. *God, I just ask three things. Let Stasia die at home. Let her go gently and easily. And let just Alsie and me be there . . . like it was at the beginning.*

He didn't tell anyone about his prayer. But in his mind it was faith's last chance. Either God came through on this, or Brian would conclude that God had turned His back on him, and Brian would then turn his back on God forever.

Brian looked back at the scene, tears glinting in his eyes. Inside he knew one more of those eternal transactions that seemed to be made weekly in our lives had just happened. He sincerely hoped God would come through.

The respite the doctors won for Stasia that evening was short-lived. The next night the bleeding was worse than ever. The arteries on Stasia's wrist began gushing again. Brian and I worked into the late-night hours, taking turns holding our fingers over the flow and stopping it.

Every time we took our fingers away from the wounds, the bleeding started again. It looked like a losing battle.

And again the doctor, this time a man, was unsure of what more he or his staff could do. He called Dr. Freeman. "Is there anything else we can try?" he asked him. "The only time it seems to stop is when the parents are there applying pressure on her wrists."

Dr. Freeman answered, "So let them stand there and apply pressure."

"All night?"

"It'll give them something to do." This was not the callous comment of a pure pragmatist, but rather words from the heart of a man who understood Brian and me better than any doctor there. He knew that giving us something to do was far better than our standing by and being impatient about the proceedings.

The doctor hurried back and told Brian and me what Dr. Freeman had said. For a moment we could laugh, even as we continued pressing wearily on the hemorrhage points. Dr. Freeman once again proved to be the ultimate realist.

Then at 12:30 P.M. the bleeding stopped again. It had been a grueling trial, certainly the worst in Stasia's short life, and both Brian and I flung ourselves into chairs to rest.

After blinking back his own weariness, Brian said, "Alsie, go home and get some sleep. I'll stay here. I can go right to work from here in the morning, if all goes well."

"I won't leave," I insisted.

"Look, if anything changes I'll call you immediately. But we can't kill ourselves with this. That would leave Stasia where?"

Looking into Brian's determined eyes, I finally agreed. "But you have to call me immediately if anything changes."

"I will."

I sped home, eager for a rest and praying that the bleeding truly had stopped. Nonetheless, two minutes after I'd crawled into bed, the phone rang. It was Brian. "It's started again."

"I'm on my way."

We worked all night, and early in the morning Dr. Freeman arrived. This time he decided to try a remarkable gel, very new, something he called "human glue." He larded the bleed points with the gel on Stasia's wrists, then wrapped them in bandages. Halfway through he turned to the legion of doctors surrounding him. "Anyone have a quarter?"

Someone immediately pulled a coin out of a pocket. Dr. Freeman set the quarter over the worst part of the wound and wrapped again. Then he tied Stasia's hand over her head on the bed.

By noon the bleeding seemed to have stopped completely. Then at 3 P.M. Dr. Freeman unwrapped the bandage with the same group of doctors present. He reached the quarter, and there was still no flow. When it was completely unwrapped, no blood showed. The group cheered. Then Dr. Freeman flipped the quarter back to the young doctor who'd given it to him. "Sometimes the old ways are best," he remarked. The residents just grinned and stared in awe as he winked at me and left the room.

That evening as I was waiting for Brian to return from work, I sat in the darkened hospital room watching Stasia sleep fitfully. Dr. Freeman's miraculous skill and imaginative thinking had stopped the bleeding, but for how long? Would tonight be a repeat of last night? How long before our little girl's heart would give out from the strain?

"Lord," I cried out in my mind, "I'm so very, very tired. How long must we endure this?" And then, like sudden lightning across a summer sky, it hit me! How long indeed! I remembered what I had said to Lil—"I'll never be able to let her go. Not unless she is suffering horribly in the hospital." Oh, how those words came back to haunt me now! So this was what Lil had meant when she said I had no idea of how bad it could get. Suddenly I knew what I had to do.

Corrie Ten Boom once said, "The things that are the most precious to us, we should hold the loosest. For it hurts when God pries our fingers free." Was God preparing me for Stasia's departure? Was He prying my fingers free? In the twilight of darkness of that quiet hospital room I lowered my head, closed my eyes, and prayed the hardest prayer of my entire life:

"You win, Lord. I can't fight You anymore. And I surely can't bear to watch my little baby suffer like this any longer. She is so very, very precious to us, Lord, and I cannot bear that one so innocent should suffer such pain. But she's precious to You too, Lord. I guess I can't keep her and protect her forever. So, Lord . . . if You could just let me take her home one more time, to her own nursery, to lie in her own crib, to be around familiar things, and let me hold her one last time, for an hour, a day, or even a week, I'll let her go, I promise. Amen."

That evening passed without incident, and the next morning Dr. Freeman stopped in to see us.

"How would you like to take Stasia home?" he asked.

I virtually leapt out of my chair and shouted, "Today?"

"Not today, but maybe the end of the week—say, Friday or Saturday."

My mind began working overtime, and Dr. Freeman caught the look on my face. He knew false hope when he saw it. "Hold on a minute, Alsie. Stasia has suffered a life-threatening illness and miraculously survived. But she's in very fragile condition. She came close, but now she's fighting. I can see her fighting—maybe only for each of you. But for now I think she's going to make it."

Brian and I threw our arms around each other and began to cry.

Dr. Freeman said, "All I've done is buy you a little time."

"I know, but that's all I asked for—a day, a week, an hour. You always could pull a rabbit out of the hat, and I love you for it."

He hugged me in one of his famous bear hugs and walked down the hall.

Talk

A COUPLE DAYS AFTER THIS, Dr. Freeman asked if we would agree to talk to several of his students. Brian said, "Sure," knowing he didn't have to say a word because I'd do all the talking.

The next morning Dr. Freeman came by and asked us to come down to the conference room where his five students were. He told them as we all sat around a conference table, "I want you to be exposed to how parents of profoundly handicapped children feel and think." He proceeded to ask us many questions about Stasia and her circumstances. It impressed both of us that he felt it was so important that his students get that kind of training.

At the end of the session we went back to Stasia's room. Several minutes later Dr. Freeman brought two of the students there as well. He said, "Alsie, there's one question the doctors wanted to ask you but didn't know if it was appropriate to do so. They wanted to know whether knowing what you do now, would you have aborted Stasia?"

I didn't hesitate. I said, "I have no regrets. If I had it to do over again, I'd do it again in a minute." I snapped my fingers emphatically. "The time with this child has been the single most fulfilling period of my entire life. I can't speak for other mothers, but for me this child has provided a greater level of depth and meaning and clarity as to what's really important in life than anything else ever has or, I venture to say, ever will." I paused for a moment, still thinking, then continued, "You know, it's funny, but three years ago when our daughter was born, my greatest fear was having a hand-icapped child. And now, almost three years later, my greatest fear is what I am going to do without her."

One of the doctors, a young black man, walked over to me, shook my hand, and looked warmly into my eyes. He said, "Thank you for your willingness to share that."

Dr. Freeman put his arm around my shoulder, winked at me, and said, "Thanks." Then they all left.

*

A couple of nights after that, Brian's parents visited us and Stasia in the hospital and volunteered to sit with Stasia while we went out to dinner. We went to Little Italy in downtown Baltimore. I was doing a lot of thinking about what life would be like without Stasia. Her passing now was a real possibility to me.

I said to Brian, "What meaning and purpose will my life have . . . what will Stasia's life mean once she's gone? When people saw her and touched her, their lives were transformed. They gained a real understanding of God's peace. But after she's gone, all of that will disappear."

Brian looked at me intently. He paused, then spoke precisely, slowly. "What about Jesus?"

"What do you mean, 'What about Jesus?'"

"What if His disciples had felt the same way you do now? Think of it this way—Jesus had a ministry on earth that lasted almost three years. During that time He touched many people's lives. But after He died, if His disciples had felt like you do, they would never have gained the power to transform the entire world, and even history."

I was stunned. Here was a man who had been having an ongoing three-year battle with God, and now he was instructing me about God's purpose in Stasia's life.

Brian continued, "Stasia's life could actually have a greater impact on people after she's gone than while she's here."

When we got back to the hospital room, I reflected on Brian's comments. I would think about that conversation many times over the next few years.

Home

TRUE TO HIS WORD, Dr. Freeman allowed us to take Stasia home on Sunday. Brian briefly wondered about his prayer, but his mind commented, *Couldn't be.*

That first week Stasia remained fragile, and I worried that every day might be our last. No one had really expected her even to leave the hospital. But now at home she slept most of the time. I lived in her room. The Good Sams from church, a group of women named for the "Good Samaritan" who were dedicated to giving help to families in need, brought meals each day.

After that first week things headed downhill again. On Sunday, March 4 Stasia began choking and wheezing and turned blue. We put her back on oxygen. By Tuesday her skin was mottled from poor circulation. Then another sinus infection struck.

I told Brian, "This is going to happen over and over until she dies." Pauline Chisholm, Chapelgate's secretary, happened to call from the church that afternoon. I poured out my feelings to her, and Pauline listened sympathetically. Then I said, "Pauline, you've been asking me for years what to pray about this. I always answered, 'Stamina.' I never asked for healing. But now I know. Pray that God puts an end to her suffering—either way—by complete healing or by taking her. Personally, I'm holding out for total healing. But I don't think that's the way it will be."

Still, I knew my "grip" on Stasia had tightened, and I didn't want to let her go. I believed intensely that "grip" had something to do with prolonging Stasia's pain.

Pauline answered, "God has a way of honoring that prayer."

We all knew the end was near, and without telling me, Brian prayed again that God would allow only the immediate family to be present when Stasia left this world. His conviction increased that this was his ultimate test of God's love. If God would grant that, he would follow Christ again—joyously.

From Your Arms to My Arms

O N SATURDAY, MARCH 10, relatives were visiting Brian's parents in Alexandria, Virginia, and when Lil volunteered to watch Stasia even though it was her day off, we considered taking the trip. It was early afternoon. Just before Lil arrived, though, Stasia's breathing grew increasingly labored. She was down to about seven breaths per minute.

I called Dr. Freeman, and he described the breathing as "chain stoking," which doctors use to describe that desperate drawing in of air in a rasp and holding it as if it were the person's last. I asked Dr. Freeman if Stasia was dying. He answered, "Yes."

I asked him how long it would take.

He said, "Sometimes weeks, sometimes days, sometimes only hours. We will pray for hours."

I hung up the phone and turned to Brian. "We're not going to Virginia." I then called Ron Steel at home, and his wife, Jenny, told us he was out jogging, but she would go get him. When he got on the phone, he said he'd be right over. In the meantime Lil had arrived, and we gathered in Stasia's room. Stasia had not been awake all that day. When Ron arrived, I was sitting in the rocker holding Stasia. Brian, Lil, my mother, and Ron gathered around me and Stasia. Ron said, "Let's pray."

A few minutes later, during Ron's prayer, I happened to open my eyes. I looked down at Stasia, and her big beautiful blue eyes were wide open. I whispered, "She's awake!" Then I added, "I'm sorry, Ron, to interrupt your prayer like this, but she hasn't been awake all day. I think your prayers have been answered."

Each one of us said something to Stasia as she looked into our faces, and then moments later, her eyes closed and she was back asleep. Ron finished his prayer and said, "Call me if anything changes."

★

At that point I knew, as only a mother can know, that my time with Stasia was now very short. And that awareness made me determined to share every last moment of it with my darling daughter. I would not forfeit one instant with this precious gift from God—not one! So later that evening, close to midnight, Brian, Lil, and I moved our home ICU into the master bedroom. I held Stasia and turned the lights down. We had endured days and days of nervous battling with pneumonia, bleeping monitors, shallow breathing, and a slow heartbeat. None of us had much hope. Shortly after midnight Stasia opened her eyes again. Although she was rarely able to focus them, as I sang songs to her she suddenly flashed that beatific smile of hers, then closed her eyes and slept peacefully. I was exhilarated.

Letting the joy saturate me a moment, I prayed, "Lord, I'm so tired. Please don't let me fall asleep. Don't let me miss a moment. I want every second with her that I can have."

I placed Stasia on the bed, lay down next to her, and promptly fell asleep from exhaustion. When I awoke, it was 4 A.M. Stasia's breathing was down to two breaths a minute. Just then all the anger of the past three years exploded from deep whithin. I began to pound my fists into my knees and to shout, "Why are You doing this, God?" The words were no sooner spoken than all of that intense rage I'd held on to for so long *vanished*. It left as quickly as it had surfaced, leaving me shaken and disoriented.

By 5:30, Stasia's breathing was down to only one breath a minute. Brian was asleep in the guest room, and I ran to wake him up. I said, "I think you'd better get in here—she's getting ready to go home." He was already getting out of bed when I arrived because he said he'd heard a loud noise. But there had been none.

We ran back into the master bedroom, and I asked Brian to put Stasia on my lap as I sat on the rocking chair. He sat on the edge of the bed next to us, holding Stasia's hand.

It was 6 A.M. and the darkness was just beginning to fade around the shades in our room. I listened to Stasia's heartbeat through the stethoscope. It was slow, shallow, almost imperceptible. And it stopped beating! Suddenly, as if struck with a lash, I realized what was really happening, and I became hysterical, crying, "Brian, she's going—she's really going." Brian began crying as well.

Instantly Stasia's eyes popped open. The tiny girl stared directly at me with that liquid blue intensity. It was so startling that I calmed down immediately. It was as if she understood what was happening and was saying, "It's all right. Everything's under control." When I was calm again, Stasia closed her eyes and slept. Her heartbeat had returned.

Moments later her heartbeat began to slow until . . .

Suddenly, in my mind's eye, the room was flooded with brilliant, white light. It was as if I were looking into a large tunnel. At the far end were two large strong male arms draped in white garments and extending toward me as if waitng for something—or someone. I was seated at the other end, and I knew who was in the middle—Stasia. Instantly I knew what the symbolism meant. Despite all my earlier promises, it was again a tug-of-war. I still did not want to let Stasia go. For over two and a half years I'd believed we would beat this handicap and Stasia would grow up healthy—perhaps a bit slow, but even if she had disabilities, we would work through them together. I'd believed I could be one of those mothers who despite incredible odds had led her child on to glory, a shining example to doctors everywhere of what love and commitment could do. When those hopes were dashed, I'd simply prayed for stamina. Finally I'd sought to see the good in it all. And God had answered in so many ways.

But to let go? To truly give Stasia up? "From your arms to My arms." It was too much to ask.

Yet, I knew it had to be. As I cradled Stasia in my arms, again her heart stopped, I began to cry, and Stasia's eyes opened wide once again, and her heartbeat came back, as though offering one last gift of her understanding and compassion. Even though I knew the baby couldn't understand, I finally said to her, "Sweetheart, Mommy is really upset. But I'll be okay. You're so tired. It's time for you to go. God is calling you. Listen to the voice, honey. Follow the voice, and go lie down in the flowers."

I felt as if I were personally placing Stasia's hand in God's hand.

Stasia rarely wept during her last two years. She was always a peaceful, placid, happy child, rarely expressing even the most guttural complaints through crying. But at that moment one tear slid out of each of Stasia's clear, blue eyes. Later Brian would say one was for me and one for him, perhaps the only way she had of saying good-bye.

At 6:10 A.M. on Sunday, March 11, just as the sun was beginning to rise, her little heart stopped beating. It was only Brian, me, and Stasia at the end, as it had been at the beginning. She was gone. God had answered Brian's prayer. He now considers it the day, hour, and second of his true conversion to faith in Jesus Christ. God had met him at his deepest need.

Separation

THE FIRST PERSON I CALLED was Dr. Freeman. He was asleep, but his wife woke him. Immediately Dr. Freeman said, "Do you want me to come out?"

I answered without hesitation, "Yes, please." Then I stopped. "No, it's all right . . . I don't expect you . . . No, please, we need you here . . . No, I'll understand if you can't . . ."

Dr. Freeman's compassionate smile seemed to touch me through the phone. He said gently, "Alsie, I'll be there as soon as I can. Just give me directions. We'll have a party—we'll have a great time."

Next I called Dr. Strahlmann. He advised me that I had to call the police. I knew I couldn't do it, and Brian was downstairs getting my mother up. The doctor said, "I'll handle it, and I'll be out as soon as I'm dressed."

After that I called Brian's parents, then Lil Price, and finally Ron Steel. Within a half hour the house was full of friends, relatives, doctors, and policemen. When Dr. Freeman did arrive, he brought with him a tiny plant—I always wondered where he'd gotten such a thing at that hour in the morning. Once he saw we were in good hands, he took his leave. Stasia was in my arms as I sat in the rocker. I knew I had to give Stasia up, but I could not seem to face that moment, and no one else seemed to know what to say or do to help me.

Pastor Steel had an eight o'clock service, but he stayed as long as he possibly could. I watched him finally depart from the bedroom. But as if a voice had spoken to him, he suddenly stopped in midstride. People were crowding around him, talking, asking questions, but Ron—a man of great compassion and seemingly infinite concentration—suddenly turned and looked at me. Instantly I knew what he was thinking, and I steeled myself for a fight. He said, "Excuse me—there's one more thing I have to do."

He strode across to me and sat down on the bed by my rocker. I began sobbing, saying, "No, no, please don't make me . . ."

Ron spoke in gentle, low tones about Stasia being with the Lord, saying this was the day of her graduation. She was not there anymore. She was with God now.

Even now I don't quite remember what Ron said, but somehow his words, as if selected by God just for me, helped me break that physical bond. I came to believe that Ron in some divine way understood what I was going through more than anyone else ever did or ever would. I would come to find out later that he indeed did.

Ron left, and then Brian began walking toward me. I knew this was truly the end, and I still didn't want to face it. But Brian knelt by me and said, "This is Daddy, Stasia. I'm here now, and I want to take you into my arms." He reached slowly for Stasia.

I said, "No, Brian. No, I won't . . ."

But Brian kept speaking, as if to Stasia. "This is Daddy, honey. Daddy's here—it's OK. So don't be afraid."

Reluctantly I gave Stasia up to my husband, and he took her out. When he reached the doorway, the breaking of the bond hit me in a way I could not have anticipated, and I screamed, a deep, soul-splitting cry that erupted from the amputation I had just suffered. I fell out of the rocker, and a friend, Carolyn DiVirgilio, who was sitting on the bed, grabbed me and pulled me up into her arms. Holding me, we wept together.

That morning when Ron finally started the church service, he announced all that had happened, and then he said, "I know some of you will think this is really a blessing that this little girl has finally had her graduation, and in some ways it is. But not for Alsie and Brian, at least not today. When you have a child like Stasia, severely handicapped, you pour so much more into the relationship; you give so much more to a child like that because she needs it, so that when she finally does graduate, it's like losing a part of your body. You can have no idea how much greater the bond is in those situations—and you must pray for them because of the separation that is now going on in that home."

I didn't hear those words until months later, through a friend. I had just told her that losing Stasia was like an amputation, and the friend related what Ron had said. It was a confirmation of much that would happen in the next few days, for Ron alone seemed to understand what Brian and I were feeling.

Finding a
Final Spot

DURING THE FOLLOWING DAYS God pulled out all the stops in ways that both Brian and I now call miraculous. Despite the spiritual nature of so much of my and Brian's journey with Stasia, the intense effulgence of grief that slammed me in those first hours was something I was unprepared to deal with. The question that pursued me doggedly was, what was the purpose of it all?

The first job, of course, was to locate a burial site. That Monday after Stasia went home to be with the Lord, Brian and I set out in search of a cemetery. In my mind this had to be an exceedingly beautiful place. I knew I'd be spending a lot of time there. I felt terribly low at that moment, realizing what we had to do, and a mental battle took place inside me.

I spoke to the Lord silently as Brian drove.

I know this probably doesn't matter to You at all, Lord. You probably think it's all very unimportant—Stasia won't be in that place, she's with You. But it's so important to me, to help me feel at peace. Just grant me this one wish, please.

I kept visualizing this picture of ducks and a pond. I'd never seen anything like it over the three years previous when occasionally

Brian and I visited some local cemetery on a drive. But the image kept returning to my mind, and I knew that was something like what I wanted for Stasia's final resting-place on this earth.

We visited a cemetery close to home, but we both knew right away it was all wrong. It stood at the intersection of two main thoroughfares. We knew there would always be so much traffic, it would be impossible to create a semblance of inner peace.

Brian drove on to a second cemetery that the funeral home had recommended. Inside the cemetery sales office, though, things were such a mess, we almost turned to leave without talking to anyone. Then a man stopped us and led us into the sales office. There a small, spry, older woman with an austere manner stood to greet us after tripping over the waste can.

When Brian told her we were looking for three plots, she radiated genuine excitement.

I explained, "We'd like to put the baby in the middle plot, between us."

Instantly the woman projected horror and dismay. "Oh no, you can't do that!"

"What do you mean, 'I can't do that'?" I answered, looking to Brian for support. We had thought about this a long time, and even sensed some people might think it strange, and this was how we wanted it. However, I had not expected this response from the salesperson.

"It just isn't done," the woman informed me with certitude. She gazed at me over her glasses, nodded with finality, then showed us some memorial markers that proved her point. They were "double markers" that clearly left no room for a third name.

I stared at this person, rather nonplussed, and my ire was rising. "We'd really like to have three plots with Stasia between us. Is there some kind of cemetery etiquette about this that we don't know about?"

Brian restrained a laugh, but the woman was adamant and suggested we go out and look. Shrugging and giving me a look as the woman turned back to me, Brian motioned for me to just go along with it. We could leave afterwards. I was upset, though, and mumbled to myself, "This is absurd, absolutely ridiculous. Cemetery etiquette! Honestly!"

We took a tour in the salesperson's disorderly, paper-strewn car. As the woman drove, she spilled out numbers and figures on the cost of each type of plot. "Over here," she said enthusiastically, "are the 450's. And over there"—she gestured in great sweeping motions, just missing Brian's head—"are the 550's."

I was seething, though Brian looked as if he thought this was great standup comedy.

Finally the woman cried with an almost indecently chipper tone, "And here we have a special two for one sale!"

When the car stopped, I simply opened the door and got out. Brian followed.

"We're leaving this place," I told him, out of earshot. "Get us out of here, I don't care how. I wouldn't have Stasia here in a million years."

Brian managed to sign off with the woman, and we went back to our car. I felt frazzled and upset, though later that day we would laugh about it together.

Brian said with understanding, "Do you want to try one more?"

I was crying now, but I nodded. "One more."

We later arrived at a tidy but wide-open place called Meadowridge Memorial Park. From the road it looked more like a park than a cemetery, and it had a large white turn-of-the-century house/office in the center of the grounds. There were great flowing oaks and firs and elms and poplars, and instantly I liked it even though I was still recovering from the previous experience. The office was prim and neat, traits I've always valued, and a very kindly elderly lady talked to us. She had no problem with Stasia being placed between us.

Then she took us for a tour. We drove up a hill, and the moment we came over it, my eyes popped open with wonder. Before us lay three ponds and about a billion ducks and geese! Streams fed the ponds, and there were small stone bridges linking them. It was a beautiful picture of the peace and tranquillity I had longed for, the exact image I'd had in my mind for Stasia's final resting-place.

Uttering a silent prayer of thanks, I knew this was it.

Nonetheless, back at the office the lady looked for three plots in a spot near the duck pond. But she could find only two open plots. I began praying almost hysterically in my mind. *This has to be it, Lord. It had to be Your choice. Please don't let it fail.*

Suddenly I noticed a pinked-in area on the map with precisely three spots. "What about that?" I asked.

The lady peered at it. "Hmmm. That was sold. But maybe . . ." She checked it. "Ah," she said, "the people who bought it canceled out only a week ago. The place is yours if you want it."

Brian and I left amazed yet again by God's provision in our lives.

A Special Song

I ALSO HAD A SPECIAL DESIRE about what would happen at the memorial service. I wanted an elder from Chapelgate, Don Speake, a tall robust man with a background in opera and professional singing, to perform "How Great Thou Art." We both went over to Don's home and talked to him about it. He agreed so long as I promised not to look at him as he was singing. "I'd burst into tears," he said.

Then I said to Don, "I don't know whether you'd know anything about this, but about twenty years ago there was a movie on a special program called 'The Student Prince.' In that musical there was a scene in which the prince's father died, and the prince stood beside the casket in full dress uniform and sang a song. That song has stayed with me all these years. Every time I've ever been in a new church, I've always looked in the hymnal to see if I could find it. But I never have. I only remember one line from it: 'I walk with God.'"

Don laughed. "That's the name of the song. And as a matter of fact, I sang that part years ago in a play!"

I stared at him. "Why isn't it in any hymnal?"

"It's not a hymn."

"Well, it's exactly what I want for Stasia."

Don shook his head sadly. "I don't know the words or the key anymore. And it's too late to send to New York."

My heart sank. But suddenly Don brightened. "Maybe I have it somewhere in the house or the car. Let me look."

He went out to the car where he kept a stash of hymns, spiritual songs, and all the music he kept available for singing in the many groups, choirs, and bands he had been part of over the years. He searched hard too, but it wasn't among the pile of sheet music he had in the backseat. Then he checked the piano bench. It wasn't there. Finally he looked in the family room. It wasn't there either. Don shook his head and sighed.

Billie, Don's wife, suddenly said, "Remember that lady back in high school . . . she became the musical director of a Methodist Church in Brooklyn Park—Ruthie Collins? She was the one who directed you in the play."

Don's brow wrinkled. "That was forty years ago, honey. And anyway, now she's married."

"Yes," Billie persisted, "but I know they moved to Brooklyn Park, and she married a man named Frank Holbrook."

I jumped up, my excitement building. "Let's get the phone directory."

They found the exchange for Brooklyn Park, and Don found three Holbrooks under Frank or F. The first one they called wasn't home. The second one said it was a wrong number—their name wasn't Holbrook. The third one answered, "Yes, this is the Holbrook residence."

Don said to the man who answered, "I don't know if you're the right person, but about forty years ago in high school I was in a play called 'The Student Prince,' and the director was Ruth Collins. We think she married someone named Holbrook and that she lives in Brooklyn Park."

The man laughed. "That's us."

Don stared at me in abject amazement. Ruth Holbrook came on the line, and Don said, "I bet you don't know who this is." He explained about the play. "You don't remember the obnoxious guy in the lead role, do you?"

The woman laughed. "Of course I do—Don Speake!"

"It's been forty years!"

They chatted for a moment, and then Don said, "You wouldn't happen to have a copy of 'I Walk with God,' that song from the play?"

Ruth thought, then called to Frank and asked him to check in several *Reader's Digest Songbooks* she had of old songs. Frank found it.

Don was speechless for a moment. But his throat quavered out the words, "What key is it in?"

Ruth told him. It wasn't the precise key Don needed, but it would do. Frank explained how to get to their house.

The fact that it wasn't quite the right key troubled Don, though, and he decided to call another friend, Alice Everhart. She had directed Don and others for over eighteen years in a musical group called The Alleluias. Alice told Don, "You have the music, Don . . . In your *Alleluia* book. But I have an easier version."

And it was the right key.

Alice gave him two copies of the music, and he would later sing "I Walk with God" at Stasia's memorial service. This was for me another marvelous confirmation of God's love, providence, and compassion.

A Fitting
Memorial

B Y THIS TIME both Brian and I believed that God was doing
something incredible in our lives beyond everything else
that had happened. Even in our grief, something was happening inside us—in fact, in many people. I knew once again there
was purpose in Stasia's life, perhaps a greater purpose than even
many of those who made headlines in her generation.

We thought long and hard about what we would inscribe on
Stasia's grave marker. One of our favorite verses was Matthew
18:10. In the context, Jesus' disciples were arguing about who was
the greatest among them. Jesus called a little child to Himself and,
placing the child on His lap, said, "See that you do not look down
on one of these little ones. For I tell you that their angels in heaven
always see the face of My Father in heaven."

We settled though on a similar passage from Luke 9:48—
"Whoever welcomes this little child in My name welcomes Me
and whoever welcomes Me welcomes the One who sent Me—for
he who is least among you all, he is the greatest." We chose that
verse because in the eyes of the world Stasia was certainly one of
the least among us, and yet her impact was far greater than anything we could have imagined.

Finally, I had requested that the following poem be read at Stasia's service. I'd gotten it from the Pediatric Neurology floor at Johns Hopkins. I took it home and personalized it for Stasia, adding a few of my own lines. It goes like this:

A Tribute to My Little Daughter

My dear little Stasia,

I've known so many joys with you,
   Though many bittersweet,
I know that through the love of God
   He made my life complete.

For He sent from Heaven, an angel,
   And He kept your little crown,
Knowing you'd return there,
   Once you left this earthly ground.

He looked for a family loving and giving,
   A home that was patient and kind,
For parents who knew their reason for living,
   That's who He had in mind.

So you were wrapped in a shining star,
   And down the rainbow you came,
A breath of Heaven here on earth,
   Our Stasia you became.

There were to be many trying moments
   When you were so sick and small,
But our love for you gave us the strength
   To see you through them all.

Stasia's Gift

You never truly had the chance
    To run about and play,
But your love in return was worth it all
    As we watched you day by day.

While other children ran and played,
    Your joys sprang all anew,
For other little angels came,
    To play those times with you.

I know that some will never see,
    Why He sent you, so meek and mild,
But I have felt God's love for me
    Through you, my only child.

So you see, my dear little Stasia,
    Through the smiles, the joys, and the tears,
We'll always be thankful and grateful,
    To have known you through the years.

You are the rainbow of my life,
    My sunshine, my spring flowers,
You're everything beautiful put into one
    That came to fill my hours.

I believe you're a very special child,
    And to Heaven you hold a key,
I believe your reason for coming here
    Was to help make a pathway for me.

A FITTING MEMORIAL

So for every little smile and tear,
 That you have given me,
God smiled and sent me you, my love,
 My key to Heaven you'll be.

> *I love you so much,*
> Mommy
> February 1990

The Most Amazing
Event of All

THAT AFTERNOON BEFORE DARK, when everyone except family had gone, I asked Brian if we could go out to visit Stasia. He readily agreed; he felt the same way. We came downstairs and told the remaining family members we were going out for a drive.

No one said anything, but as we stepped out the door, Brian's mother called, "Aren't you going to take some bread for the ducks?"

I thought, *We can't get away with anything around here.* But it made my spirit soar.

As we drove out, I thought about my life now without Stasia. For thirty-five years I had struggled to find some purpose and meaning for my life. When Stasia was born, I discovered that meaning and purpose. She was everything and more. Loving and nurturing her had filled this aching vacuum in my soul. Later, when I realized I had a personal relationship with Jesus Christ, I realized part of that ache was my own need for God. But God had filled that vacuum first with Stasia and then through her led me to a deeper understanding of Him and His ability to meet all my needs.

Now, though, all I could see were endless lonely years without

Stasia, without purpose, without meaning, with nothing of what I had gained through Stasia's coming into my life. The depression seemed to engulf me during that ride to the cemetery, and I repeatedly asked myself, *What am I going to do now?*

When we'd left the cemetery that morning, Stasia's coffin stood over the grave. There were flowers all around it. There had been a multitude of people. I remembered how I had told Stasia during those last few minutes together, "It's time to go lie down in the flowers."

But now as we parked and I looked toward the spot where Stasia lay, everything had changed. The tiny gold and white casket with the four angels on the corners was gone. The grave had been filled in. Only flowers covered the spot.

The feeling of desolation was so intense, I was not sure I could even walk to the site. What hit me was the finality of it all. That morning I could still reach Stasia in some tangible way. I could see her and touch her. But now I saw she was truly gone. I would never hold Stasia again. I would never see her face, listen to her first cry in the morning, dress her, or do anything else that I so treasured. There was no sense of eternity, no hope of Heaven, no conviction that Stasia was with Jesus. The picture I'd had that morning of Heaven and hope and Stasia lying down in the flowers—all that had fled. All that was left was the searing pain in my heart of the finality of it all. Our life together was truly over. The distance between us now seemed eternally unbridgeable—as if Stasia and I were now light-years apart. It was a pain so sharp, so final, so complete and overwhelming that I felt abandoned and alone again in the universe. *Where are You, God? Why have You left me?*

With the gathering dusk and the ducks and geese bedding down for the night, it was still the idyllic setting I had hoped it would be. All was quiet. We talked quietly, and Brian kept reiterating his need of me as his wife and best friend. As we stood at the grave site I looked down at the flowers. Brian put his arms around me, and again we sobbed for several minutes. Despite Brian's reassurances, the desolation inside me deepened.

Fifty feet away stood a little stone bridge over a waterfall between two of the ponds. Golden sprays of sunlight hung on the western horizon. Though this was March, the past few days had been unusually warm in Maryland. But with night coming, there was a chill in the air. The warm spell was passing.

Brian and I walked hand in hand to the other side of the bridge. We stood there a moment, and then suddenly we both felt a soft, warm breeze envelop us. It was like walking over a grate in the city during the winter, with the warm air shooting up around you. Startled, I peered down at the ground to see if there indeed was a grate or an underground opening.

But there was nothing.

I extended my arm. My fingertips were cold. Inside they were warm. I stepped out of the circle of air. Cold. I stepped back in. Warm.

What on earth was this?

I looked at Brian, and we both froze. There was a long pause as we each struggled to comprehend this strange sensation. Finally I said hesitantly, "Did you feel that?"

Brian had a mystified look on his face. He slowly responded, stretching out the word as if he were questioning too. "Yeah."

We continued walking on around the ponds. Neither of us spoke, but we were both preoccupied with what had just occurred. Perhaps it was some strange weather phenomenon, like a downdraft of some sort; or perhaps the strain of the last few days had just been too much. As we rounded the last pond, we rang a set of chimes, then meandered back to the grave site. It was getting dark very quickly, and the temperature was dropping. I hugged myself inside my coat, the air on my face making me wish I had a scarf.

At Stasia's grave, again we held one another tightly and sobbed.

As fresh waves of grief washed over us, suddenly the warmth was there again. This time, though, it was stronger, more tangible.

I knew it was not just a breeze or an updraft. It felt like human breath—gentle, sweet, enveloping—but above all, intimate. It was just like the moment before kissing Brian when I could feel his breath on my cheek and we embraced. The chill seemed to vanish, and I stepped back from Brian. Instantly I felt enfolded in a divine Presence.

The Presence seemed to embrace me, and an indescribable sense of rapture seized me. I felt as if I were rising off the ground, higher and higher. A feeling of excitement—no, ecstasy—gripped me. There was no sense of time. It seemed to go on and on as if time had ceased to exist. The ecstasy built and built, and the sensation of rising took me higher and higher. All anxiety was gone. Fear had vanished. As if I were climbing the first and greatest peak on a giant roller coaster, the excitement at what was ahead only enlarged. And yet, it was such an intense joy that I realized no human body could possibly contain it, and in another moment I would die. Yet, there was no fear of that unknown but only a joyful greeting. The emotion billowed and enlarged until I knew I could not hold it one second longer. At the precise moment I felt death was imminent, the feeling of rapture slowly diminshed.

Slowly, gently I felt lowered back to earth, and a moment later I found myself firmly planted on the ground, looking into Brian's eyes and wondering if he had experienced any part of what had just transpired.

Brian swallowed and blinked. We embraced again, but we didn't say anything. A few minutes later we went back to the car.

For the next day I didn't think about anything but that experience. I wondered if I was going through the nervous breakdown I had anticipated before Stasia's passing. Two questions were paramount in my mind. First, why had Stasia been born, and why did she die? Why had God brought her into our lives only to take her away? God had sent us a beacon, a light to guide us safely to Him and then introduced us to an intimacy with Him we'd never had before. She had been the beginning of everything I had yearned for. It was as if God gave me a purpose for living and then yanked it all away. Why? It made no sense.

But above all was the second question: if on the other hand it all meant nothing all along, if there was no purpose in it all, if it was just a "stroke of fate," why had God given us that experience at Meadowridge and provided such powerful assurance and hope?

Moses struck me as the primary example. He was going to save his nation, be the man of the hour. Then he murdered an Egyptian and ended up living as an exile for the next forty years. I wondered, *Am I supposed to wait until I'm seventy-five years old before God will begin to work in my life again?*

It was all a terrible paradox in my mind.

Early the next morning Pastor Steel called and wanted to know how we were doing. Both Brian and I were on the line, on extensions. I told Ron what had happened at the cemetery, hoping he would assure me I was not losing my grip on reality. Even more, I hoped he would give it all some meaning.

After spilling out the whole story, I said, "Well, what do you think? Have I finally gone off the deep end?"

There was a long pause. Finally Ron answered, "No, I don't believe so, Alsie. What took place out there I believe you can find in Matthew 28:20. That verse says, 'And surely, I am with you always, to the very end of the age.' God was trying to reassure you that indeed He has not abandoned you, and indeed you are not alone, and that although the next few months are going to be very difficult, He will be with you every step of the way. With all my heart I'm convinced He was giving you something to hold on to, something real and tangible to help you cope with the emotions you have and will have. He was assuring you, 'I am with *you* always, Alsie and Brian, to the very end of the age.'"

"So you think it was real?"

"Yes." He paused, then said, "Remember this, Alsie—God never wastes suffering. He's going to use what you've gone through for good in ways you can't possibly expect. He's going to do more than you've ever imagined. That's the way God always works in the lives of His children."

He paused again. Finally he said, "There's a great quote I've often thought about: 'Those whom God uses greatly, He wounds deeply.'"

Immediately I knew Ron was right. At Meadowridge, in that hour when the finality of it all came down on me and I felt most alone and most abandoned, He had come to me in a way I could not deny.

Although at that moment I still had questions that would not be resolved for years, there would be many times over the next few months when I would mull over the purpose of my and Brian's and Stasia's lives. Frequently I would be tempted to wonder if I was not just forcing all these ideas on my own situation as a way of coping when in reality I was no different from any other mother of a handicapped child. My mind would say to me, "Who are you to think there is purpose in this? Why should you think you are anything but just another mother of a handicapped child who lived and died?"

When those thoughts would strike, I would always return to that moment in Meadowridge when I knew God had reached out to me, embraced me, and assured me He had created me for things beyond even Stasia's entrance and exit from my life. It was a short, fleeting moment, and yet it clearly affirmed our new relationship and His presence in our lives.

✳

That afternoon Ron's wife, Jenny, called and said, "I'd like to get together with you on a regular basis."

I really had had no close friendships or relationships for the three years of Stasia's life, and I had only met Jenny the day of the funeral. So I asked her, "Why, considering your busy schedule, would you want to do that?"

She said, "Well, I've often struggled with depression since we've moved up here. I've had to start over in many ways, find new routines and new friends and everything else. But I found that regular exercise, gospel music, and working to build new friendships have helped a lot. So basically I'd like to get to know you. Is there a day that would be good for you and me to just talk and be together for a while?"

I said, "Pick a day. I have no plans." I really didn't know where to begin in going back to leading a normal life, but Jenny's commitment and love encouraged me. Jenny finally picked Wednesday. During the next year Wednesday became a focal point of my life. Sometimes I'd show up at the Steels' home at 9 A.M. and stay until evening, with Brian arriving for dinner. It became our sole anchoring point on a sea of constant change that first year. Because we had that "home base" of love and support, we found the courage to begin living the life God intended for us.

The grief wasn't gone. Maybe it will never completely disappear. But something eternal had been offered beside that tiny grave at Meadowridge. I received it as one more mark of God's great love.

An End and a Beginning

THE NEXT FEW DAYS WERE A STRUGGLE. Brian had sprouted spiritual wings with his conviction that he no longer had only an intellectual understanding of Christ and the gospel. He possessed a deep belief in a personal God who had suddenly become an intimate friend. He saw now that what was required was a genuine and complete dependence on God for everything, and he sensed that he had taken that first major step. He also sensed a powerful inner forgiveness from God for the last few years of anger and bitterness. Above all, he believed he shared with God the intimate feeling of having lost your only child. It was for him an exhilarating, inspiring insight.

I, on the other hand, plunged into the depths of a depression worse than anything I'd faced during Stasia's short life. I wept at all hours and was sometimes up all night. I kept every article that was part of Stasia's "retinue" in place. I didn't know what to do with my hands, since I was so used to holding Stasia. And I carried one of Stasia's toy animals with me everywhere I went.

That Friday, two days after the funeral, I sat trying to drink my cup of tea and fight back the waves of darkness that crashed over me. Mornings were especially bad. That had always been Stasia's special time with me, and even with Lil still coming each morning to spend some time with us, the memories flooded over me like stormy surf. I began praying that God would take me to Heaven to be with Stasia once again.

As I sat staring around the room, knowing that God was not going to do what I asked, wondering if I could survive the emptiness of a life without Stasia and without purpose, I noticed Stasia's medications tray. On it sat a full bottle of chloral hydrate, the same sedative once used in the classic Mickey Finn era when thugs killed one another off through an overdose of the drug in a cocktail. When I saw the little bottles, a voice seemed to whisper, "You have a way out."

I told myself, "If it gets too bad, I'll do that."

Somehow the idea comforted me.

Lil arrived later that morning. After getting settled, she came in and sat with me. There was a funny, insightful grin on her face. She said, "I have something to talk about with you, Alsie. But first I want to ask—is there something you want to tell me?"

I realized that Lil might know my thoughts, and I answered, "Lil, I don't want to talk about anything."

Lil replied, "I'm a nurse, Alsie, and I have a duty. I know what goes through a woman's mind at a time like this."

"What are you talking about, Lil?" I stared at her insistently, trying to play dumb, though I knew what she was referring to.

Lil gestured toward the drug tray. "The chloral hydrate, the phenobarbital . . . You know they can be used for things other than seizures."

I immediately said, "You know I wouldn't do anything like that." I tried to fix her hard with my eyes, affecting a sincere, determined stance, but Lil just shook her head.

"I want to throw all the medications out," she said with finality.

"It can wait," I insisted again, watching my only comfort on earth begin to evaporate. "What's the big deal?"

"No . . . I want to do it now."

Brian was standing at the sink, and he walked over to me and sat down. Placing his arm on my shoulders, he said, "I think we should throw it out now, honey. I agree with Lil."

"It's not necessary . . . I'm . . ."

But Lil and Brian were already moving toward the sink. A few seconds later, as they poised to pour it all down the drain, I nodded with resignation. It made me feel even more depressed, my one ray extinguished. But I knew they were right.

Lil sat down with me again. "I know you don't want to do what you were thinking about doing, Alsie," she said. "You'd break God's heart."

She said it with such conviction that I swallowed hard. At the moment I didn't know what I believed about God anymore. I was back to the old roller coaster, and all the changes and learned lessons of the last year looked like a fantasy.

Lil touched my hand. "I know what it feels like, Alsie. But the Lord loves you. He will see you through this, if you let Him. He will heal you, too. Give Him the same chance He gave you with Stasia."

It was a powerful exhortation, and I nodded, hoping I would find the words true.

Later that morning I started my devotions. I usually read from three devotionals as the pattern of my quiet time—*Our Daily Bread*, published by Radio Bible Class; *Morning Cheer*, a pamphlet issued by WRBS, a local Christian radio station I often listened to; and *Daily Guideposts*, a book of readings put out by *Guideposts* magazine. I went to the readings with despair in my heart, wondering if God would have anything to say to me today.

I began reading mechanically, barely paying attention to the text. The first one finished with a verse from Psalm 27: "Wait for the Lord. Be strong and take heart and wait for the Lord" (verse 14).

It seemed an apt word, but I didn't know how I could do it. I turned to the next devotional. To my surprise, the title began with the same quote: "Wait for the Lord." The text spoke of the need to learn to give God time to work in your life.

I stared incredulously, wondering how this could have happened. But I told myself I really didn't think that meant anything. I knew from experience Psalm 27:14 was a favorite text of devotional writers.

Then I opened the third devotional. The same text stared out at me: "Wait for the Lord. Be strong, and take heart and wait for the Lord."

That verse and Romans 8:28 and Matthew 28:20 became my texts for the next two years of struggle. During this time there were so many people, events, and experiences that strengthened Brian and me as we were both forging a new life in a world without Stasia.

Often I simply wanted to give up. Life had been so much simpler when Stasia was with us—not easier, but simpler. Goals were clearer, values more easily distinguished. Now it seemed, in her absence, that life was easier but so very much more complicated.

We felt our primary purpose during Stasia's brief lifetime had been to help people see the wonderful gift this child was to us, that she had been sent by God, that she had a purpose in life, that she was not some horrible fluke of fate or some dreadful accident, but was rather the best thing that had ever happened to us. She had come into the world ill-equipped to handle life's storms and trials, or so we thought. But we were wrong. Her feet were planted on earth, but she was ever Heavenbound. She was so filled with the presence of God that she could not help but overflow onto whomever she met. It is an awesome experience to meet such a gift from God.

True, she couldn't walk, talk, sit up, or care for herself in any way. She would never go to college, grow up to raise children of her own, or become president of Citicorp. However, countless people—Christians and non-Christians alike—have testified to the spiritual impact she had on their lives after only a few minutes with her. Again and again she touched hearts and souls. We used to describe her as a Rolls Royce trapped inside an old dump truck. The outer vehicle was a mess, but inside she was pure gold. She taught us about what was truly important in life, about values, about God and about having a meaningful relationship with Him. She taught us about time and how to use it, about people and about a whole segment of the population we knew nothing about or even cared to—the handicapped. She taught us about unconditional love, total dependence, absolute trust, and loss of control—or rather, who really holds the reins. She taught us about parenting and about the inestimable value of human life. And on and on . . .

It was all such a life-transforming experience and in many ways still is. But the question remained, "What now, Lord? What do You want me to do now?" So much had happened, so many miracles . . . Surely we were being prepared for something, but what? About the time I was wrestling with these questions, four things occurred that would eventually answer all of my questions, and even a few I hadn't thought to ask.

The first two happened shortly after Stasia's departure. I had two dreams. In the first I was standing in a room all alone—no other people and no furniture or other objects. A beam of light was coming from above, surrounding me with its brilliance. My arms were at my side, and my face was lifted up toward the light.

The second dream had no people in it at all, not even me! All I saw was one of those old-fashioned ice cream soda glasses—very tall, very thick, with ridges on the side, sitting on a glass base. The very wide top tapered down to a narrow bottom. The glass was sitting on a table, and water was being poured into it from some unknown source above. The odd thing about it was that when the glass was filled, the water didn't stop. It just kept coming and coming, and the glass continued to stand upright but was overflowing with the abundance of water.

I pondered these dreams for many days and, unable to come up with any plausible explanation, finally called Reverend Ron Steel.

He explained to me that the dreams' meaning were basically this: In the first dream my position—arms at my side, face uplifted, eyes closed—was one of submission to the light, God's will. The second dream seemed to relate to John 7:38—"Whoever believes in me, as the Scripture has said, streams of living water will flow from within him." The two dreams together seemed to be saying that as I would submit to God's plans for me, an abundance of blessing would flow through me.

"What *is* His will?" I asked Ron.

"Ah, that's for Him to reveal to you," he responded.

"When?"

He chuckled. "When He's ready—in His own time."

So I waited and waited and . . .

One day, exactly a year after Stasia's homegoing, I was sitting in the nursery, sobbing bitterly and feeling very much alone. Suddenly, in intense rage and frustration, I raised my hands toward Heaven and cried, "Why don't You just let me die!"

Instantly I heard that familiar still, small voice: "Because I want more for you." That's all. Just "Because I want more for you." I stopped crying, but I could have used a little more information, if you know what I mean.

That was occurrence #3, and it kept me going, like Moses in the wilderness, for another year.

A year later things weren't looking any better. Brian and I had been hoping and praying for another child and were undergoing fertility tests, but so far without success. We'd even explored the adoption option. But, though we were very excited about this at first, God made it clear to us this was not His will for us. I can't explain how we knew, but we just knew.

On top of that, Brian decided to not pursue the fertility tests any further, saying he knew in his heart that God was not leading us in that direction. I wasn't so sure, but, recognizing that Brian was the spiritual head of our household, I acquiesced. For the first time since Stasia's homegoing I was faced with the possibility that we might never have other children. All I could think was, "What is life without children?"

So it was that I took my burden to the Lord on the second anniversary of Stasia's departure. I'd always assumed the role God had for me was that of mother. Wasn't that Stasia's purpose in coming—to introduce me to such a life? God kept reassuring me and giving me new hope, but when were things going to start moving? That very day I asked God, "If not motherhood, what?"

He directed me to go back and reexamine those almost three years with Stasia. I told Him I'd already done that, but He made it clear that I should do it again. I did, and this time I saw more than the mother/daughter relationship. This time what struck me was the concept of having a significant impact on another human being's life, caring for them at a time when they need you most and actually improving the quality of his or her life, no matter how brief that life might be. The message was suddenly clear to me: *nursing*.

I couldn't believe it! Me a nurse? I get sick just thinking about blood! But God was serious! I ran downstairs and told Brian that God wanted me to be a nurse, and he burst out laughing. "Are you sure you heard Him properly? Perhaps you should ask Him to repeat what He said, just in case."

When we sat down to talk about it, however, we came to the conclusion that I had nothing to lose. It wasn't as if I had anything else pressing to do. Besides, I'd probably flunk out the first semester. But I promised God I'd pursue it until He shut a door in my face.

A year later, having been accepted into the Johns Hopkins School of Nursing for my Bachelor of Science in Nursing degree, I was carrying a 4.0 average. What do I know anyway?

✳

So often in the almost three years that we were able to share with Stasia, people would ask us, "How do you do it?" or they'd say, "We're so sorry for you. We can't imagine what it would be like to lose our only child; watching her deteriorate little by little over a period of three years. How do you keep your sanity?" Funny, there was never enough time to ponder that question while she was with us. But now that she's home with God, I've had plenty of time to contemplate that question and hopefully come up with some answers.

How did we do it? How did we survive? How did we cope? Oddly enough, *we* didn't. At least not alone. God was there to supply all that we lacked and more—so much more than we ever dreamed possible. I used to tell people that as surely as they knew that if they took a flying leap off a tall building, they wouldn't sprout wings and fly, *I knew* beyond a shadow of a doubt that I could not raise a handicapped child. I knew it in my heart as surely as I know my name. And I was right. I couldn't. But God coud. And thus it was that I came to know God as El Shaddai, the All-sufficient One. Nothing in my entire life had even remotely prepared me to cope with caring for a handicapped child. I had neither the patience, the fortitude, the commitment, the knowledge (from a medical or maternal standpoint), the stamina, the insight, and worst of all, even the interest to raise such a child. In short, I was sadly lacking in all respects. And yet, time and time again I sat bemused while someone told me of their admiration for all the patience, the fortitude, the commitment, the knowledge (from a medical and maternal standpoint), the stamina, the insight, the dedication and love that as a parent they could see in our relationship with Stasia. Over and over I would ask myself, Whom do they see? I knew for a fact it wasn't me. I loved to hear about this person who seemed to have taken my place; but just as surely I knew it was not me.

What then made the difference? LOVE. And yet more than love—*unconditional* love. I'd heard about it. Goodness knows, I'd read about it often enough in church or Sunday school or in the Bible; but what was it really? I thought I knew, mentally at least. I mean, when you really sit down and think about it, when have you ever *personally* experienced it? Try as we might, as human beings condemned to walk in sin for our earthly lives, when has anyone ever shown you *unconditional* love? Or for that matter, when have you shown unconditional love to anyone? The very word *unconditional* is irrevocably linked with the concept of consistency. Thus unconditional love is not a now-and-then or once-in-a-while occurrence. By its very nature, unconditional love must be reliable, constant. So then, how does one *experience* unconditional love? The answer, I was to learn, is through God. For He and only He is capable of loving us unconditionally or giving us the gift of unconditional love. My lesson came wrapped in pink, with ten tiny toes and ten tiny fingers and two of the bluest eyes you've ever seen. Yes, I believed I loved her unconditionally—never asking or seeking anything in return. My heartfelt desire was simply to be allowed the priviledge of caring for her for the rest of *my* life. I simply never wanted it to end.

That's what God can do for you. He can take your deepest fear and turn it into your greatest victory. It is not simply a matter of no longer fearing the thing; one is actually brought to the place where you actually crave the very thing that caused you paralyzing terror in the past. Now *that's* a miracle! The very thing that had previously terrified me, having experienced it with God beside me, supplying my needs, now became the single most fulfilling experience of my life. For one brief moment that lasted almost three years I was permitted the luxury of experiencing God's unconditional love. And in loving my only child in this way, I came to understand how very much God loved me—a sinner. So this was what they meant by unconditional love!

Sometimes God's gifts last for a lifetime. But often He shows us what He wants, allows us to experience it so that we have a better understanding of what it is, and then, as a loving parent must, He slowly and ever so gently stands back and allows us to stand on our own, developing and nurturing the gift and learning from the experience. How do I know it was a gift? Simple—not once before she came into our lives, nor, despite my most ardent efforts since she's been gone from our lives have I been able to duplicate that love. I've tried, oh how I've tried, and more often than not, miserably failed. But each time perhaps I get a little closer, until that time when I can stand before my Father and thank Him for the privilege of loving one of His very own. "Let the little children come unto me, and do not hinder them, for the kingdom of God belongs to such as these."

And so in the end, on March 11 at 6:10 A.M. just as the sun was rising on the Lord's Day, I did not hinder this little one from returning to her Heavenly Father, the Author and Creator of unconditional love. And we try to honor her memory by practicing the lessons she and God taught us—lessons of trust and peace, peace of the soul and peace in the midst of discord, total surrender to God's will, comfort in sorrow, strength in weakness, light in darkness, and love—unconditional love. (And that might come in pretty handy as a nurse, don't you think?)